Teaching World History Through Wayfinding, Art, and Mindfulness

Teaching World History Through Wayfinding, Art, and Mindfulness

Amber J. Godwin

ROWMAN & LITTLEFIELD
Lanham • Boulder • New York • London

Published by Rowman & Littlefield
An imprint of The Rowman & Littlefield Publishing Group, Inc.
4501 Forbes Boulevard, Suite 200, Lanham, Maryland 20706
www.rowman.com

86-90 Paul Street, London EC2A 4NE

Copyright © 2024 by Amber J. Godwin

All rights reserved. No part of this book may be reproduced in any form or by any electronic or mechanical means, including information storage and retrieval systems, without written permission from the publisher, except by a reviewer who may quote passages in a review.

British Library Cataloguing in Publication Information Available

Library of Congress Cataloging-in-Publication Data

Names: Godwin, Amber, 1981- author.
Title: Teaching world history through wayfinding, art, and mindfulness / Amber J. Godwin.
Description: Lanham, Maryland: Rowman & Littlefield, 2023. | Includes bibliographical references. | Summary: "Teaching World History Through Wayfinding, Art, and Mindfulness approaches world history instruction through standards-based arts- and story-telling prompts"—Provided by publisher.
Identifiers: LCCN 2023034248 (print) | LCCN 2023034249 (ebook) | ISBN 9781475870619 (cloth) | ISBN 9781475870626 (paperback) | ISBN 9781475870633 (ebook)
Subjects: LCSH: History—Study and teaching.
Classification: LCC D16.2. G57 2023 (print) | LCC D16.2 (ebook) | DDC 907.1—dc23/eng/20230821
LC record available at https://lccn.loc.gov/2023034248
LC ebook record available at https://lccn.loc.gov/2023034249

Contents

Foreword		vii
Preface—Just Open Your Eyes and See That Life Is Beautiful		ix
1	Livin' on a Prayer . . . in a Cave	1
2	Desperately Wanting: Identity-Forming in Classical Civilizations	17
3	Immigrant Singing: Movement and the Post-Classical Era	33
4	In the Renaissance, My Name Is Human	51
5	The Beginning Is the End Is the Beginning: Colonization and Empire	61
6	Raging Against the Machine: Industrial and Democratic Revolutions	75
7	Bullets and Butterfly Wings: Investigating Imperialism	87
8	Standing Alone: Pre- and Post-World War I	97
9	The Space Between Our Wicked Lies: The Great Depression and World War II	109
10	Frozen Remix: Navigating the Cold War	123
11	Am I Wrong for Thinkin' Out the Box from Where I Stay? New Identities, Decolonization, Revolutions, and Revolutionary Impacts	133
Conclusion—We are the People We've Been Waiting For		143
About the Author		147

Foreword

Ask just about any adult what they remember about their middle- or high-school history classes, and they will probably roll their eyes and answer, "Labeling and coloring maps, memorizing dates and facts, and being tested on it." Occasionally someone might answer that they enjoyed their history classes because they had a teacher who made it come alive for them; and these responses would be in the prodigious minority. Yet, history (and all the social sciences) have the potential to be the class or subject that people remember long after their school days have ended; and remember for positive reasons. Long ago, when dinosaurs roamed the earth, a high school history teacher changed my life because he got me to think—really think—for the very first time in school (a much-belated thank you, Mr. Hines). I remember thinking of it as a powerful gift: to influence another person to think. Later, I discovered that Socrates said *he could not teach anyone anything, that he could only make them think*, and this, too, inspired me. That set me on a track to become a social studies teacher myself and ultimately to work with preservice teachers in higher education. I bring my sordid past up to illustrate that reaching impressionable minds and having an impact on them is not only feasible, but imperative, especially in the social sciences. If we are to believe the prognostications of what future skills will be needed by our students, critical and creative thinking will be first and foremost.

Dr. Amber Godwin suggests two highly important contexts that should be considered when teaching world history: art and mindfulness, and both lend themselves to critical and creative thinking. In her book *Teaching World History Through Wayfinding, Art, and Mindfulness*, she makes a compelling case for history teachers to go beyond the old Maps-Dates-Facts mindset. Both can facilitate and inspire students to employ critical and creative thinking, and the events or era become meaningful and relevant.

The arts are at the heart of understanding a people or society. Their values and the core of their being are reflected in their music, literature, and visual arts. For students to make sense of the past and reflect on the present and future, they must have an understanding of the people involved. If the student has something of interest to which to tie the information, learning occurs and the arts, or a specific component, definitely is of interest to them. After all, history is literally his-story. It is one thing to recall an event or date, but true learning takes place when the material is meaningful and relevant, and ways that teachers can make instruction significant are included in this book.

By paying attention to the arts when studying world history, mindfulness is an organic result. Through the lens of the arts, the student will be able to view people and events as if for the first time in a humanistic way rather than as facts and figures. Seeing parts of an event, era, or people that might otherwise be overlooked is crucial for students to make sense of what they are studying. This is something that educational philosophy and pedagogy has stressed for as long as there have been "best practices." In short, thinking outside of the box can come naturally to them rather than as something to be remembered to do.

In this book, Dr. Godwin gives insightful and practical guidance on establishing a world history classroom in which critical and creative thinking are the emphasis. Should facts, dates, and figures be eliminated entirely? Certainly not; they will always play a role in the study of the past. However, they should not be the focal point, but rather ancillary pieces to help students grasp the whole or big picture. At its core, *Teaching World History Through Wayfinding, Art, and Mindfulness* helps teachers guide students to see the past through a different lens of the arts and mindfulness and encourage deeper understanding. Socrates, and Mr. Hines, would approve.

—William D. Edgington, Ed.D.

Preface

Just Open Your Eyes and See That Life Is Beautiful

After many years as a social studies teacher, I came to the awful conclusion that there is no corner in the timeline of history where we can collectively huddle, safe from the violence of humanity. Still, violence is not the complete story of where and whom we come from, and that should not keep us from seeking out the good in our past. Our ancestors had creativity, imagination, innovation, passion, and curiosity. They had good days and bad days, they celebrated, they mourned. They had complex lives, just like we do, and they expressed themselves through personal and cultural pathways (Sherman & Morrissey, 2017), through art. When we consider art, we may not always feel safe, but we can relate, and that is where I found the common thread—in the stories, in the art, of our collective past.

That is where I wanted my class to be situated, in a space where we all could connect without fear, but with curiosity, a place we could all engage. That kind of engagement requires students to be involved in the learning, co-constructing experiences in the classroom with the teacher and with each other. In approaching this kind of active learning, we can practice historical empathy (Berry, 2021; Lovorn & Dristas, 2017; Mirra, 2018; Newstreet et al., 2019), which can support a more mindful exploration of who we, and our students, are in the now (Ling, 2021).

As a teacher/scholar, I find most of my inspiration for engaging lessons through a process of wayfinding (Howard & Kern, 2019; Page-Reeves, 2019; Symonds et al., 2017), seeking art that tells the story of history that helps activate empathy toward a shared human experience. Storytelling provides an organic avenue to exploring one's personal and cultural identity (Bruner, 1990; Godwin, 2021) even beyond the top of the cultural iceberg (Hall, 1976). After all, personal cultural exploration was once seen as a critical method of instruction (Howard, 1991).

Stories have been used to teach lessons (Briody et al., 2012) and paint pictures in the minds' eye, because "words are images too" (Burmark, 2002, p. 19). Therefore, stories will also be included in the discussion on art throughout history. Indeed, allowing students time to share their own ideas and stories (Lantheaume & Letourneau, 2016; Levesque & Croteau, 2022; Levy, 2014) can further empower students to learn from each other (Ladson-Billings, 2021). By making space in the classroom to "engage students' historical ideas, attachments, and identities" (Levesque, & Croteau, 2022, p. 120), there is also a found place for the practice of mindfulness in the classroom (Jin, 2022).

Sōtō Zen monk Suzuki said that the practice of mindfulness is important, "so wisdom could be various philosophies and teachings, and various kinds of research and studies" (Suzuki, 1970, p. 111). But *mindfulness* has also been defined as the cultivating of the mind's ability to see everything as if for the first time, abandoning judgments and opinions to see parts of something that might otherwise be overlooked (Suzuki & Dixon, 2010). Thiền Buddhist monk Thích Nhất Hạnh defined *mindfulness* as "the miracle by which we master and restore ourselves" (1975, p. 14), stating that it "enables us to live" (Nhất Hạnh, 1975, p. 15). Nhất Hạnh later expanded the necessity of mindfulness with regard to relationships as a way to find our own self-awareness in greater communities:

> Nothing can exist by itself alone. It has to depend on every other thing. That is called inter-being. To be means to inter-be. The paper inter-is with the sunshine and with the forest. The flower cannot exist by itself alone; it has to inter-be with soil, rain, weeds and insects. There is no being; there is only inter-being. (2002, p. 47)

It follows then that bringing mindfulness into the classroom reinforces traditional best practices from education philosophers by creating student- and community-centered (Freire, 1993; Shockley & Cleveland, 2011; Tuhiwai-Smith, 1999; Vygotsky, 1978) classroom experiences that are meaningful (Vygotsky, 1978), enriching, and transformative (Dewey, 1938). In other words, good teaching naturally, organically, fosters mindfulness. There will be suggestions for mindfulness practice mentioned at the start of each chapter that are adapted from activities expressed by Nhất Hạnh, Chödrön, and others.

Effectively engaging in history through mindful consideration of art fosters the authentic exploration of content while also providing a medium for character and interpersonal development, including critical social and emotional learning (Garner et al., 2018; Henderson & Hursh, 2014; Ladson-Billings, 2021), a necessary component of today's curriculum. There is a developing body of research on mindfulness practices benefiting those with depression as they reflect on personal past experiences (Isham et al., 2022). These studies have identified strategies that can be applied here regarding education about our collective past:

> The less-beneficial strategies that they reported on included: a) trying to avoid thinking about past events, b) thinking about past events in an evaluative and judgmental way, c) trying to suppress emotions when thinking of past events. The more-beneficial strategies included: a) changing the way they thought about the situation, b) being able to think about the memories without having to react to the thoughts and feelings. (Isham, 2022)

These findings provide an excellent framework for the goals of this text, to help address the past in a way that acknowledges, while teaching healthy strategies to confront and process the emotions that can come up as topics are being discussed. Furthermore, emerging research has found that engaging in mindfulness activities about the past can also promote reflection on the present and future (Niedderer et al., 2022). Mindful consideration of events can even help spark cognitive flexibility, a component of creativity (Richardson et al., 2022). Allowing for mindfulness situated in a formal pedagogy can cultivate life skills that will serve students far beyond their time in our classrooms.

Additionally, supporting social-emotional learning (Weissberg, 2019) through mindfulness practices provides a chance for students to deconstruct their internal responses to things as they are learning content and "gaining deeper self-knowledge" (Sensoy & DiAngelo, 2017, p. 13). This again supports the development of historical empathy by encouraging students to begin thinking critically (Berry, 2021; Mirra, 2018; Newstreet et al., 2019) about experiences of others from the past (Strupp-Levitsky et al., 2020). Furthermore, recent evidence suggests that nurturing mindfulness is a life skill that can enrich the quality of life and quality of relationships for those who practice it (Reina et al., 2022). These characteristics are needed for our students to grow to be healthy citizens, to support them as they become more aware of themselves, but also to be more empathetic (Hanneke Bartelds & van Boxtel, 2020) in today's increasingly global (Fitzsimons, 2019; Magazzini, 2017; Vertovec, 2007) communities.

My goal was to create a text that provides a road map for telling stories of world history through art. But what is art? Some Native American traditions, including the Shoshone, find art everywhere, in both the process and product of art, which can be useful or ceremonial (Kulei Nielson, 2022). Tolstoy (1902) claimed mankind would not exist without art, and Ayn Rand said that art is a selective re-creation of reality (1975). Bentz et al. (2022) said, "the humanities and the arts can connect us with the innate knowledge that our senses reveal about an ever-changing world." Those perspectives co-construct pieces of the lens through which art will be examined in this text.

My father once said, "Art is when you appreciate something for what it is; science is when you continually experiment with something to extrapolate what it has the potential to be," and that is one idea. But artists like da Vinci and Picasso make me wonder if there is more complexity to this issue than we have previously given credit to, as if art and science are two sides of the same coin, like the Greek tradition of recognizing the sameness of Apollo/Dionysus (Broad, 2007), and whether acknowledging that might unlock a greater truth. This hypothesis has been offered and explored previously and is being revitalized by scholars (Baldacci & Guaraldo, 2022), and artful expression through science (Bentz et al., 2022) will at times be explored in this text because countless lessons on the history of science find congruent themes to those addressing art in history.

So, art is process, art is a perspective, and art is a science. Again, it seems that any over-complexation or oversimplification of art can prove dangerous. For the purposes of this text, the definition of *art* will align adjacent with Weitz (1956) in that it will not be defined because "no matter how we define art, new art can be created which poses a counterexample to the definition" (Baldini, 2022, p. 2). Here, the art that is discussed in the text will be determined based on what is discovered through wayfinding.

Although *wayfinding* does not have a fixed definition, components include (a) interweaving dynamic dwelling and (2) creating possibilities, through (3) emergent perspective and (4) experiential wisdom (Page-Reeves, 2019, p. 183) and is "the cognitive, social and corporeal process and experience of locating, following or discovering a route through and to a given space" (Symonds et al., 2017, p. 15). The route we are looking for here is a way to provide tangible stories of world history through pieces of art that can help teachers construct learning experiences that promote social studies understandings while practicing mindfulness.

I hope this text provides a useful thread of historical context, including arts-based content and stories, suggestions for mindfulness engagement, and ideas for how to formatively assess student understanding. I hope you find this mindfulness, story, and arts-based approach to teaching world history to be valuable, along with the suggestions for art as an instructional assessment tool (Donovan & Anderberg, 2020; Swift & Godwin, 2021) that will utilize student skills (Freedman, 2006) to help them practice the social and emotional intelligence needed for personal and interpersonal development (Ladson-Billings, 2021). I hope reading, considering, and applying the ideas in this text sparks your curiosity about the past, about yourself, and about the collective in which you find yourself. I hope you find this exercise to be meaningful and transformative to your teaching practice. I hope that together we can find a way to look beyond the broad strokes of human history to find the humanity beneath, and that what you discover or affirm is that life is beautiful.

References

Baldacci, C., & Guaraldo, E. (2022). Archiving the anthropocene: New taxonomies between art and science. *Holotipus, 3*, 17–22.
Baldini, A.L. (2022). Philosophy of street art: Identity, value, and the law. *Philosophy Compass, 17*(9), 1–12.
Berry, S. (2021). *How the implementation of video games in education could result in higher accessibility, empathy, and critical thinking skills in the education system* (Unpublished thesis). Texas State University, San Marcos, Texas.
Bentz, J., do Carmo, L., Schafenacker, N., Schirok, J., & Dal Corso, S. (2022). Creative, embodied practices, and the potentialities for sustainability transformations. *Sustainability Science, 17*, 687–699.
Briody, E., Pester, T. M., & Trotter, R. (2012). A story's impact on organizational-culture change. *Journal of Organizational Change Management, 25*(1), 67–87.
Broad, W.J. (2007). *The Oracle: Ancient Delphi and the science behind its lost secrets*. Penguin.
Burmark, L. (2002). *Visual literacy: Learn to see, see to learn*. ASCD.
Chalmeh, R., Fouladchang, M., Jowkar, B., Fazilat-Pour, M. Investigating the mediating role of mindfulness in the relationship between autonomy supportive environmental and critical thinking in students. *Journal of Psychological Science, 20*(107): 1965–1978.
Dewey, J. (1938). *Experience and education*. Touchstone.
Donovan, L., & Anderberg, S. (2020). *Teacher as curator: Formative assessment and arts-based strategies*. Teachers College Press.
Fitzsimons, S. (2019). Students' (inter)national identities within international schools: A qualitative study. *Journal of Research in International Education, 18*(3), 274–291.
Freedman, K. (2006). *Leading creativity: Responding to policy in art education*. UNESCO World Conference on Arts Education. Lisbon, Portugal. Retrieved January 12, 2021, from https://wayback.archiveit.org/10611/20160106222015/http://portal.unesco.org/culture/en/files/29857/11386135391kerry_freedman.htm/kerry_freedman.htm.
Freire, P. (1993). *Pedagogy of the oppressed*. Continuum International Publishing Group.
Garner, P.W., Bender, S.L., & Fedor, M. (2018). Mindfulness-based SEL programming to increase preservice teachers' mindfulness and emotional competence. *Psychology in the Schools, 55*(4), 377–390.
Godwin, A.J. (2021). Stopping the persistence of memory: Creating cultural inclusivity in the classroom. *Universality of Global Education Issues Journal, 8*(1).

Hall, E.T. (1976). *Beyond culture* (1st ed.). Anchor Press.

Hanneke Bartelds, G.M. Savenije, & van Boxtel, C. (2020). Students' and teachers' beliefs about historical empathy in secondary history education. *Theory & Research in Social Education, 48*(4), 529–551.

Henderson, J., & Hursh, D. (2014). Economics and education for human flourishing: Wendell Berry and the oikonomic alternative to neoliberalism. *Educational Studies, 50*(1), 167–186.

Howard, G.S. (1991). Culture tales: A narrative approach to thinking, cross-cultural psychology, and psychotherapy. *American Psychologist, 46*(3), 187–197.

Howard, M.A., & Kern, A.L. (2019). Conceptions of wayfinding: Decolonizing science education in pursuit of Native American success. *Cultural Studies of Science Education, 14*(4), 1135–1148.

Isham, A.E. (2022, October 31). The benefits of mindfulness when thinking about past events. *Psychology Today*. https://www-psychologytoday-com.cdn.ampproject.org/c/s/www.psychologytoday.com/us/blog/days-gone/202210/the-benefits-mindfulness-when-thinking-about-past-events?amp

Isham, A.E., del Palacio-Gonzalez, A., & Dritschel, B. (2022). The effects of an online mindfulness intervention on emotion regulation upon autobiographical memory retrieval in depression remission: a pilot randomized controlled trial. *Mindfulness*.

Jin, K.D. (2022). Mapping the mindfulness: A literature review of mindfulness in educational field. *Open Education Studies, 4*(1), 136–147.

Ladson-Billings, G. (2021). I'm here for the hard re-set: Post pandemic pedagogy to preserve our culture. *Equity & Excellence in Education, 54*(1), 68–78.

Lantheaume, F., & Letourneau, J. (Eds.). (2016). *Le recit du commun: L'histoire nationale racontee par les eleves*. Presses universitaires de Lyon.

Levesque, S., & Croteau, J.P. (2022). "We will continue our struggle for success": French Canadian students, narrative, and historical consciousness. *Theory & Research in Social Education, 50*(1), 101–124.

Levy, S. (2014). Heritage, history, and identity. *Teachers College Record: The Voice of Scholarship in Education, 116*(6), 2–34.

Ling, L.H. (2021). Mindfulness and motivation in self-transformation: Thich Nhất Hạnh's Teachings on the Interbeing. *MANUSYA: Journal of Humanities, 24*, 334–354.

Lovom, M., & Dristas, V. (2017). The Mt. Lebanon project: Partnering to re-envision the teaching of world history. *History Teacher, 50*(3), 331–358.

Magazzini, T. (2017). Making the most of super-diversity: Notes on the potential of a new approach. *Policy and Politics, 45*(4), 527–545.

Mirra, N. (2018). *Educating for empathy: Literacy learning and civic engagement*. Teachers College Press.

Newstreet, C., Sarker, A., & Shearer, R. (2019). Teaching empathy: Exploring multiple perspectives to address Islamophobia through children's literature. *Reading Teacher, 72*(5), 559–568.

Nhất Hạnh, T. (1975). *The miracle of mindfulness: A manual on meditation*. Beacon Press.

Nhất Hạnh, T. (2002). *No death, no fear: Comforting wisdom for life.* New York: Riverhead Books.

Nhất Hạnh, T. (2007). *Planting seeds: Practicing mindfulness with children.* Parallax Press.

Niedderer, K., Holthoff-Detto, V., van Rompay, T.J.L., Karahanoglu, A., Ludden, G.D.S., Almeida, R., Duran, R.L., Aguado, Y.B., Lim, J.N.W., Smith, T., Harrison, D., Craven, M.P., Gosling, J., Orton, L., & Tournier, I. (2002). This is me: Evaluation of a boardgame to promote social engagement, wellbeing, and agency in people with dementia through mindful life-storytelling. *Journal of Aging Studies, 60*(100995), 1–22.

Page-Reeves, J., Marin, A., Moffett, M., DeerInWater, K., & Medin, D. (2018). Wayfinding as a concept for understanding success among Native Americans in STEM: "Learning how to map through life." *Cultural Studies of Science Education, 14*(1), 177–197.

Rand, A. (1975). *The Romantic Manifesto. Second expanded edition.* New York: New American Library.

Reina, C.S., Kreiner, G.E., Rheinhardt, A., & Mihelcic, C.A. (2022). Your presence is requested: Mindfulness infusion in workplace interactions and relationships. *Organization Science, 0*(0).

Richardson, C., Henriksen, D., Mehta, R., & Mishra, P. (2022). Seeing things in the here and now: Exploring mindfulness and creativity with Viviana Capurso. *TechTrends: For Leaders in Education & Training, 66*(3), 394–400.

Sensoy, O., & DiAngelo, R. (2017). *Is everyone really equal?: An introduction to key concepts in social justice education* (Second edition). Teachers College Press.

Sherman, A., & Morrissey, C. (2017). What is art good for? The socio-epistemic value of art. *Frontiers in Human Neuroscience, 11*, 1–17.

Shockley, K.G., & Cleveland, D. (2011). Culture, power, and education: The philosophies and pedagogy of African centered educators. *International Journal of Critical Pedagogy, 3*(3), 54–75.

Strupp-Levitsky, M., Noorbaloochi, S., Shipley, A., & Jost, J.T. (2020). Moral "foundations" as the product of motivated social cognition: Empathy and other psychological underpinnings of ideological divergence in "individualizing" and "binding" concerns. *PLoS ONE, 15*(11), 1–19.

Suzuki, S. (1970). *Zen mind, beginner's mind* (1st ed.). Weatherhill.

Suzuki, S., & Dixon, T. (2010). *Zen mind, beginner's mind.* Shambhala.

Swift, A., & Godwin, A.J. (2021). Creative canvas: Engaging in arts-based formative assessment. *Social Studies Texan, 37*(1), 31–34.

Symonds, P., Brown, D.H.K., & Lo Iacono, V. (2017). Exploring an absent presence: Wayfinding as an embodied sociocultural experience. *Sociological Research Online, 22*(1). https://doi-org.ezproxy.shsu.edu/10.5153/sro.4185.

Tolstoy, L.N. (1902). What is art? In *The Novels and Other Works of L. N. Tolstoy.* Translated by Aline Delano. (pp. 328–527). Charles Scribner's Sons.

Tuhiwai-Smith, L. (1999). *Decolonizing methodologies: Research and Indigenous Peoples.* Zed Books.

Vertovec, S. (2007). Super-diversity and its implications. *Ethnic and Racial Studies, 30*(6), 1024–1054.

Vygotsky, L.S. (1978). *Mind in society: The development of higher psychological processes*. Harvard University Press.

Weissberg, R.P. (2019). Promoting the social and emotional learning of millions of school children. *Perspectives on Psychological Science*, 14(1), 65–69.

Weitz, M. (1956). The role of theory in aesthetics. *Journal of Aesthetics and Art Criticism, 15*, 27–35.

Chapter One

Livin' on a Prayer . . . in a Cave
Circa 6000 BCE–2000 BCE

Our exploration of world history begins before what is considered recorded history, with Early People. It is difficult sometimes to imagine living in the conditions they faced. Perhaps we imagine their lives to be harsher than *they* perceived them to be; for Early People, life was just that—life. It may be challenging to consider exactly what that life might have looked like, felt like, smelled like . . . but because people think in pictures (Berger, 1973), art provides us a way to try to situate our thoughts adjacent to those earliest ancestors. Art also provides a medium that begins to explore the importance of imagination, which is "transcendental in that it precedes and is necessary for the rest of our thought" (Burns, 2022, p. 6) and may have been essential to our survival (Morriss-Kay, 2010).

Suggestions for mindfulness aligned to this content are adapted from *Planting Seeds* (Nhất Hạnh, 2007, p.29).

- Questions to consider: What do you already know about this content? What are your expectations? How can you allow yourself to be open to the experience of storytelling and mindfulness?
- How to stretch into the practice of mindfulness as you read: Be aimless. Allow yourself to be open to this experience. If you are working with students, have an open area of paper around the room for them to create a mural as they are working through the lessons you adapt using the suggestions at the end of the chapter. This practice supports not only an openness to the present, but also community building and interaction.

GUIDING QUESTIONS

- How did Early People use art to express the conditions of their lives?
- How did the concept of personal property change the way society created art in the transition from hunter/gathering into River Valley civilizations?
- Did the geographic features of the six cradles of civilization impact the way art was created?
- How did social, political, and economic features impact art in the six cradles of civilization?

Early People survived through a system of migration. Hunting and gathering, movement, and permanent regional migrations were all qualities of the cycle of life that our early ancestors were accustomed to for thousands of years. These groups of people consisted of tribal bands who were constantly in search of the herd and other resources such as grains that they used to keep their families fed and safe.

During this period of transfer, several types of art have been preserved: that which has mobility and that which does not. This exploration lends itself to a series of questions that delve into our collective past, but also our individual understanding:

- What story or stories do you think Early People were trying to preserve? Why?
- Who were their art pieces for?
- How were the arts expressed?

There are no simple or obvious answers, but taking the time to unpack them can help provide a context for us to begin trying to connect with those communities and find what threads we continue to share with them through our own experiences.

Cave paintings and rock engravings (Morriss-Kay, 2010) provide an opportunity, not only for the exploration of Early Man, but also for an exploration of self. Modern thinkers try to infer the meanings of these paintings, with some discussions that branch not only into the realm of human consciousness, but also into spirituality (Maier et al., 2019). Others attest that cave paintings indicate a life where:

> survival required heightened awareness. Indeed, the cave paintings themselves are products of exactly this kind of awareness ... It also calls on resources of memory that have been built over a period of time during which animals of all kinds have been carefully observed. The hunter and the painter, like the animals portrayed, are all watchers. (McGregor, 2015, p. 24)

Both attributions indicate a desire to explore something internal, indicating an interest in further developing imagination, meaning "not simply the criteria of novelty in an 'image,' but the development of an individual into a social, cultural form of life" (Pelaprat & Cole, 2011, p. 416), which then sparks the question: Does the cultivation of imagination then lead to the start of human culture? These paintings could provide evidence that Early People were seeking a way to remember (Peirce, 1960), particularly when cultivating a community that could be bound together by shared stories (Bruner, 1990). It is also notable there is speculation that music and dance paired with these visual arts (as seen in figures 1.1 and 1.2) and the stories that were told about them (Killin, 2018). It is speculated that these special moments together as a tribe were meant to "steer away from tensions of the day to singing, dancing, religious ceremonies, and enthralling stories . . . Night talk plays an important role in evoking higher orders of theory of mind via the imagination" (Wiessner, 2014, p. 14027).

Examining these images and trying to imagine the stories they helped visualize is another component to exploring Early People that allows us to delve again into our own humanity. What might these stories have indicated? How do you think heroes were remembered? Were there any villains? Who were they? What more was not being expressed in the paintings that might have

Figure 1.1. Hands at the Cuevas de las Manos in Santa Cruz Province, Argentina; created c. 7300 BCE–700 CE.

Figure 1.2. Astuvansalmi prehistoric rock paintings in Ristiina, Finland; created c. 3000-2500 BCE.

been indicated in other, lost visual or performance arts? How did music and dance help illustrate the story? And were all those components (storytelling, visual art, music, and dance) connected at all times? Why? Why not?

It is possible that the paintings were created to entertain or to warn, but it is also probable that the stories of these paintings also addressed a primal need that humans have always had: the need for nutrition. Here in the cave painting stories, there may be tales of hunting ventures, with explanations of what worked and what didn't, primitive parables to provide hope and sustainability.

Another source of hope (Dixson & Dixson, 2011) may be found in a different form of expression by Early People: the Venus figurines. These figurines continue to be a source of curiosity for scholars who, even now, speculate on the intention of the creators (Dixson & Dixson, 2011; Weber et al., 2022). Some believe these figurines provide evidence that Early People practiced balanced male/female relationships, that women were able to maintain a high social status, and that early nomadic societies were goddess-worshiping (Gimbutas, 1974; Neumann, 1955; Stanton & Stewart, 1995). This ambiguity provides a perfect avenue for us to participate in an active inquiry.

Consider the Venus figurines in figure 1.3:

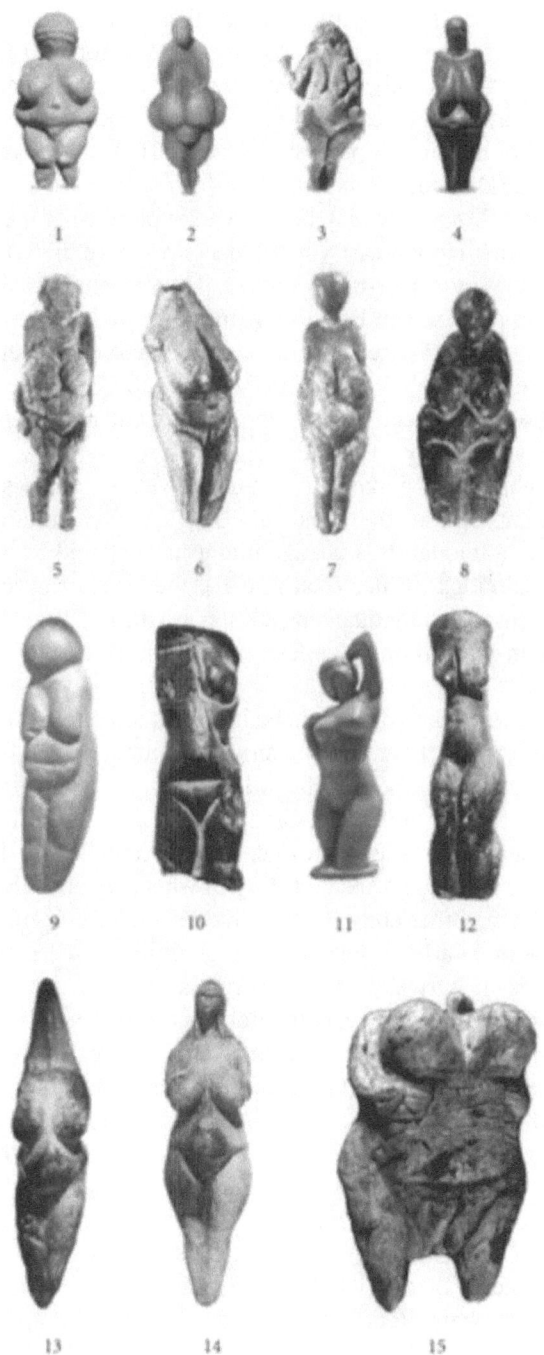

Figure 1.3. Venus figurines

You may choose to share some or all of these with your students based on your own professional judgment. As you can see, some of these are quite abstract (see #13) while others are more robust in their symbolism. Still, some students may not be ready or able to have these conversations about the symbology of fertility (Foster & Derlet, 2013) versus representations of attractiveness (Dixson & Dixson, 2011) or considerations of spirituality (Weber et al., 2022), but they may be ready to explore what these images tell them. Consider this: How might your students perceive the art? What might they see when they consider these statues? How might it make them feel? This questioning process can lead to a naturally growing classroom conversation about the cycles of the year, the cycles of life, and even connections to pop culture (e.g., "The Circle of Life" song from *The Lion King*) that can help these abstract ideas become more meaningful and more significant in the lives of your students.

It is also notable that the investigation of the Venus figurines may indicate another important shift in the tribal mindset: a movement from collective to individuation. Although this change might have started to be explored as early as cave paintings (Maier et al., 2019), the Venus figurines provide a more tangible sense of individualism (Dixson & Dixson, 2011). This progression continues in various ways as Early People moved away from hunting and gathering.

Sometimes the evidence that we have indicates large bands of tribes existing in one region for an indeterminate amount of time. For these people, their art is just as old, but because they lived in different regions, they had access to different resources, so it is understandable that they left different artifacts. Consider the Chantuto people of Mexico, who not only left seashell structures (Voorhies, 2004), but also an abstract story of what they ate, where they lived, and who they were. Other coastal sites provide similar evidence that "by the late Pleistocene and early Holocene, fishing peoples lived along coastlines, rivers, and lakes in Africa, Eurasia, Australia, and the Americas, creating shell midden soils marked by accumulations of mollusk shells, animal bones, artifacts, and other cultural debris" (Erlandson, 2013, p. 21).

The resource securities (and sometimes insecurities) of Early People came from meat and other animal products (i.e., bones, furs) that were harvested from the water or the herd, while grains like early strains of wheat, millet, oats, and barley, among others, were used to create a kind of early beer (McGovern, 2009; Wang et al., 2021) that was safer to drink than water. Over time, the burden of seeking out wild grains led tribes to start experimenting with planting seeds (Katz & Voigt, 1986), but this is a continued source of curiosity for researchers. Recent evidence suggests there may be other forms of coexisting with planting that allowed tribes—particularly in Australia—to maintain movement and plant cultivation (Veth et al., 2018) at the same time. Other tribes in Afroeurasia chose to semi-settle in one place to grow crops. In both cases, a search for sustainable resources occurred over generations of testing, observation, and assessment that for some eventually led to the establishment of permanent, fixed, agrarian, settlement-based lifestyles. Even today

> farms feed us, but what farms feed us with has for millennia been, and will continue for the foreseeable future to be, the descendants of wild plants and animals brought into the human community by Neolithic farmers and herders around the world. (McGregor, 2015, p. 296)

Civilizations rose in river valleys. These were the result of not only a dependable food supply, but also a sense of safety. For some, this reliable food supply eventually led to a food surplus, and then the question of what to do with the remaining excess from the harvest. Keeping extra food around is not only a waste of a perishable resource, but it can also lead to an increase in unwanted issues (i.e., an increased presence of scavenger animals) that then create other problems to address. Citizens saw this as a new opportunity to increase a practice they might have already dabbled in: establishing consistent trade routes and advancing transportation systems.

The distinctions of "hunting" and "gathering" indicate nomadic bands, whom we can infer traversed together with the seasons and the herds. It is more difficult to define exactly what other kinds of transportation systems (i.e., wagons, boats) Early People might have had, at least not in complete terms. Despite conflicting evidence of when exactly the wheel was invented, and by whom (Belančić, 2020; English, 2021; Menon, 1995), we know that Early People, even in the Early Bronze Age, likely not only had contraptions with wheels, but also participated in trade networks, with strong evidence indicating a healthy barter system (Mentesana et al., 2018) in practice with small goods being exchanged, including those made by metal (Childs-Johnson, 1989). This might have also been supplemented by sea trade, at least in some places. For example, "The inhabitants of the Arabian Gulf were among the world's earliest maritime traders. Their ships sailed regularly between the Bronze Age civilizations of Mesopotamia, Bahrain and the Indus Valley" (Carter, 2002, p. 44). Ultimately, having food, a permanent place to stay, and time not spent directly attending to one's survival needs led to an increase in specialized labor (including tradespeople), advanced cities, advanced technologies, and complex institutions and recordkeeping, as seen in table 1.1.

Table 1.1.

Characteristics of civilization	Mesopotamia	Egypt	China	Norde Chico	Olmecs	Harrapan (Indus)
Advanced cities: civilizations must have cities for trade	Ur, Babylon, Uruk, Sumer	Thebes, Memphis	Beijing, Anyang, Hangzhou, Nanjing, Xi'an, Luoyang	Caral	San Lorenzo and La Venta	Lothal, Dholavira, Mohenjodaro, Kalibangan
Specialized workers (examples: artisans, priests, tradespeople)	Merchants, artisans (furniture makers, jewelry makers), musicians	Engineers, doctors, scribes, nobles, and farmers	Highest-to-lowest status: scholars (which included doctors and warriors), farmers, artisans (artists and craftsmen), and merchants	Artisans, warriors, and farmers	Traders, merchants, and farmers	Farmers and craftsmen, specialized workers in complex villages included holy people and, eventually, government workers
Complex institutions (examples: ziggurats, governments)	Hammurabi Code, polytheistic beliefs	Pyramid at Giza, polytheists, pharaohs	Dynasties, Mandate of Heaven, Confucianism	Terraced pyramids, platform mounds	Giant heads, city temple complexes	Caste system, Hinduism
Recordkeeping by tradespeople, religious officials, and others	Cuneiform used by Sumerian traders in the region with people in Mesopotamia	Hieroglyphics	Hieroglyphics, oracle bones	Quipu	No written records, but extensive mathematics and calendars	We do not know much, but we know there were records kept
Advanced technology (examples: the wheel, sails, a plow)	Metal working; glass making; irrigation; use of copper, bronze, gold, and iron	Math, geometry, surveying, astronomy, paper creation, writing, metallurgy	Paper making, printing, gunpowder	Farming-irrigation, pyramid structures	Geometry, art, Meso American calendar	Standard weights and measures, carving, metallurgy

As you can see in table 1.1, in much the same way that one could define "falling asleep, slowly, and then all at once" (Green, 2012, p. 75), human development also seemed to rush forward. As trade and transportation grew, so did the need for recordkeeping. After all, a food surplus came to mean a chance to increase resource wealth, either for oneself or for one's family. Selling surplus food resources then began a need for recordkeeping—a way to indicate what was owed to whom and when. And with that began the earliest form of writing: cuneiform.

Cuneiform glyphs were markings that indicated words (Gordin et al., 2020), which eventually led to the development of an alphabet. The written word was not only a fundamental change in communication, but some believe it was also a change in the way humans thought. If "our minds are shaped by the written language in which we read" (Pae, 2020, p. xi), then written words were a progression that may have profoundly changed the way Early People created art and viewed the world (Shlain, 1998).

One way art evolved was through different kinds of stories being told, tales that were not necessarily grounded in reality, at least not all the time. And this development was important because "fiction has enabled us not merely to imagine things, but to do so collectively" (Harari, 2015, p. 25). Stories allowed people to provide a context for the way they felt, which, in some stories, provided examples for entire communities to follow. Some stories described what people believed a good ruler to be.

One of the oldest of these is the story of Sargon of Akkad. His biography—etched in cuneiform—tells the tale of his young life as an orphan child, abandoned by his changeling (some say priestess) mother, and left in a basket among the reeds until he was found and adopted by a gardener who raised him to be humble and hardworking; he also claimed to have a relationship with the goddess Inanna. This fantastical story provided justification for his rule, placing his early life in a setting and situation that seemed familiar to those who were common citizens, instead of appearing as though he came from those in power (Mark, 2014).

Some stories of leadership provided components formed of mythos and historical fact threaded together by multiple leaders—for example, the Assyrian warrior queen Semiramis (Stronk, 2017). She had a similar circumstance to Sargon in her birth, being an orphan child of the goddess Atargatis and raised to be a priestess before a series of events rendered her ruler of her people. However, the details of her rule seem to be stitched together to reflect at least two historical queens in Assyrian history rather than just one. The impact of the rulers, or in this case, the one ruler, Semiramis, has continued to influence female leadership throughout history (Asher-Greve, 2006), attesting to a celebration of the capability of women in power.

Other stories allowed for an exploration of fears—another common connection students today can feel with our collective ancestors. *The Epic of Gilgamesh* is considered by some to be "the oldest epic excavated from the earth" (Cregan-Reid, 2015, p. 3). The story explores themes of extravagance, excess, the dichotomy of civilization and wilderness, wisdom, and ultimately mortality. These themes again feel familiar, especially for students who may already be reading *Beowulf*, an interesting medium for comparison.

These representations of art in the mind's eye leads us back to a discussion of visual art in the form of monuments, representations of our humanity that outweigh the persistence of time and reinforce cultural ideologies of power. Some of these elements of power in ancient architecture include a tall height, a vast zone, a construction of stone, and the use of legends, decorations, and columns (Dehbozorgi, 2016). Ancient ziggurats and pyramids provide perfect examples of these elements, reinforcing the power of those who created them. Consider the picture of the pyramid in figure 1.4:

Figure 1.4. Pyramid

What do you think the architect of this structure was trying to preserve and why? How do you think the Nile played into the idea of the structure? How do you think people far away felt seeing the pyramid? What impact do you think it had on nearby citizens? These are all great ways to spark conversations with your students, not only about architecture as art, but here about how the environment impacted its creation, or to explore other ideas like how a structure could impact the authority of a leader.

Makeup (Parish & Crissey, 1988), hairstyling (Haas et al., 2005), clothing (Chiglintsev et al., 2019), and jewelry (Chiglintsev et al., 2019; de Beauclair et al., 2006) provide an interesting rounding out to our discussion here on art and our earliest ancestors. These self-as-art methodologies provided another means of transmitting messages of authority and opulence to others. Early civilizations found citizens wearing jewelry in an effort to project wealth and success to others (de Beauclair et al., 2006) while others saw rulers' garments or crowns as more important to defining power (Chiglintsev et al., 2019).

This chapter opened with an invitation to allow aimlessness, to be open and mindful of the present when interacting with the content. The chapter addressed how Early People used art to express the conditions of their lives, how the concept of personal property changed the way society created art in the transition from hunter/gathering into River Valley civilizations, how the geographic features of the six cradles of civilization impacted the way art was created, and how social, political, and economic features impacted art in the six cradles of civilization. In table 1.2 there are some suggestions for how to translate ideas from the text into classroom activities centered on art and mindfulness. Each of these three lesson suggestions can be adjusted to your needs as a teacher; they are intended to be a canvas that you can use to construct your lesson. Please note: these activities may take different amounts of time for different groups of students, which is a natural consequence of individual curiosity, which should be honored to keep students engaged in their learning. Remember to use your professional judgment to reduce or enrich these suggestions according to the needs of your students.

Table 1.2.

	Warmup	Suggested activities	Closing
Lesson 1.	Ask students, "What is your earliest memory?" then have them share out and discuss. Then grow the conversation by asking, "What is the earliest (or oldest) thing you know about human history?"	• Construct stations for students to visit that provide information about the lives of Early People. • Assessment: The students will create a storytelling narrative to share with the class ONE component of Early People that they think may be the basis for future social, political, and economic institutions.	• Exit ticket: The students will do a quick write on what they think the MOST important resource was to Early People and why.
Lesson 2.	Ask students, "What is ONE pattern that you see every day." Then grow the discussion by asking, "What is the pattern? What would have to happen to change the pattern? What would happen if the pattern changed?"	• Craft an inquiry lesson with visual and textual representations showing the shift from nomadic lifestyles to farming that include some of the examples above. Have students work in groups and share out. • Assessment: The students will create a pattern that represents the progression from groups of Early People to River Valley civilizations (examples: beats on a drum, bead designs, colors on visual arts, dance), then present.	• Turn and talk. Ask students if they think the progression happened quickly or slowly—then follow up by asking, "Why? Why not?" and supplement with, "How was this represented in their pattern?" Have students share out or do a "parking lot" post it to close.
Lesson 3.	Ask students, "What role does water play in your life?" Then allow for class discussion. Explain that the basic needs we have now were the same for Early People. Then ask, "How do resource needs impact our lives now? How did resource needs impact the lives of Early People?"	• Using flexible grouping, provide research stations and crafting stations for the class. Then assign each group (or individual) one River Valley civilization to discover. • Assessment: The students will create a visual representation (an "artifact") of the civilization they researched and share out, pretending to be a curator from a museum presenting their artifact to an audience.	• Quick write. The students will summarize what they learned about River Valley civilizations in ten words or less. • Pro tip: Use these summaries to start your next lesson.

References

Asher-Greve, J. (2006). From "Semiramis of Babylon" to "Semiramis of Hammersmith." In S.W. Holloway (Ed.) *Orientalism, Assyriology and the Bible, Hebrew Bible Monography*.
Belančić, A.T.G. (2020, January 6). *World's oldest wheel found in Slovenia*. Slovenia.si. Retrieved June 18, 2022, from https://slovenia.si/art-and-cultural-heritage/worlds-oldest-wheel-found-in-slovenia/.
Berger, J. (1973). *Ways of seeing*. Viking Press.
Bruner, J.S. (1990). *Acts of meaning*. Harvard University Press.
Burns, H. (2022). Imagining imagination: towards cognitive and metacognitive models, *Pedagogy, Culture & Society*, 1–20.
Carter, R. (2002). The Neolithic origins of seafaring in the Arabian Gulf. *Archaeology International*, 6, 44–47.
Chiglintsev, E.A., Bikeyeva, N.Y., Griger, M.V., Vostrikov, I.V., Ahmadiev, F.N., Zaitsev, A.A., Shadrina, N.A., & Dusaeva, E.M. (2019). Images of power in the societies of antiquity and the Middle Ages: Symbols and ritual practices of the east and west. *Journal of Politics and Law*, 12(5), 83–87.
Childs-Johnson, E. (1989). Shang ritual bronzes. In the Arthur M. Sackler Collections (Book Review). *Art Bulletin*, 71(1), 149.
Cregan-Reid, V. (2015). *Discovering Gilgamesh: Geology, narrative and the historical sublime in Victorian culture*. Manchester University Press.
de Beauclair, R., Jasim, S.A., & Uerpmann, H.P. (2006). New results on the Neolithic jewellry from al-Buhais 18, UAE. *Proceedings of the Seminar for Arabian Studies*, 36, 175–187.
Dehbozorgi, M. (2016). Recognition of the elements of power in architecture. *Urban and Regional Planning*, 1(4), 97–104.
Dixson, A.F., & Dixson, B.J. (2011). Venus figurines of the European paleolithic: Symbols of fertility or attractiveness? *Journal of Anthropology*, 2011, 1–11. https://doi.org/10.1155/2011/569120.
English, T. (2021, March 2). *Do we know who invented the wheel exactly?* Interesting Engineering. Retrieved June 18, 2022, from https://interestingengineering.com/who-invented-the-wheel.
Erlandson, J.M. (2013). Shell middens and other anthropogenic soils as global stratigraphic signatures of the Anthropocene. *Anthropocene*, 4, 24–32.
Foster, J., & Derlet, M. (2013). *Invisible women of prehistory: Three million years of peace, six thousand years of war*. Spinifex Press.
Gimbutas, M.A. (1974). *The gods and goddesses of Old Europe: 7000 to 3500 BC myths, legends and cult images*. University of California Press.
Godwin, A.J. (submitted). *Over 100 ready to use world history activities for high school*. Teacher's Discovery.
Gordin, S., Gutherz, G., Elazary, A., Romach, A., Jiménez, E., Berant, J., Cohen, Y. (2020). Reading Akkadian cuneiform using natural language processing. *PLoS ONE*, 15(10). https://doi.org/10.1371/journal.pone.0240511.
Green, J. (2012). *The fault in our stars*. First edition. Dutton Books.

Haas, N., Toppe, F., & Henz, B.M. (2005). Hairstyles in the arts of Greek and Roman antiquity. *Journal of Investigative Dermatology. Symposium Proceedings, 10*(3), 298–300.

Harari, Y.N. (2015). *Sapiens: A brief history of humankind.* Harper.

Katz S.H., & Voigt, M.M. (1986). Bread and beer: The early use of cereals in the human diet. *Expeditions, 28*(2), 23–34.

Killin, A. (2018). The origins of music: Evidence, theory, and prospects. *Music & Science, 1*, 1–23.

Maier, G.J., Musholt, E.A., & Stava, L.J. (2019). An interpretation of the famous scene in the shaft in the Lascaux cave and its connection to paintings at the cave entrance. *Journal of Transpersonal Psychology, 51*(2), 242–264.

Mark, J.J. (2014, August 30). *The legend of Sargon of Akkad.* World History Encyclopedia. Retrieved June 20, 2022, from https://www.worldhistory.org/article/746/the-legend-of-sargon-of-akkad/.

McGovern, P.E. (2009). *Uncorking the past: The quest for wine, beer, and other alcoholic beverages.* University of California Press.

McGregor, J.H. (2015). *Back to the Garden: Nature and the Mediterranean World from prehistory to the present.* Yale University Press.

Menon, S. (1995). Chariot racers of the steppes. *Discover, 16*(4), 30–31.

Mentesana, R., De Benedetto, G., & Fiorentino, G. (2018). One pot's tale: Reconstructing the movement of people, materials and knowledge in Early Bronze Age Sicily through the microhistory of a vessel. *Journal of Archaeological Science: Reports, 19*, 261–269.

Morriss-Kay, G.M. (2010). The evolution of human artistic creativity. *Journal of Anatomy, 216*(2), 158–176.

Neumann, E. (1955). *The great mother: An analysis of the archetype.* Pantheon Books.

Nhat Hanh, T. (2007). *Planting seeds: Practicing mindfulness with children.* Parallax Press.

Pae, H.K. (2020). The emergence of written language: From numeracy to literacy. In: Script effects as the hidden drive of the mind, cognition, and culture. *Literacy Studies, vol. 21*. Springer.

Parish, L.C., Crissey, J.T. (1988). Cosmetics: A historical review. *Clinics in Dermatology, 6*(3), 1–4.

Peirce, C.S. (1960). *Collected papers of Charles Sanders Peirce, vol. 2.* Harvard University Press.

Pelaprat, E., & Cole, M. (2011). "Minding the gap": Imagination, creativity and human cognition. *Integrative Psychological & Behavioral Science, 45*(4), 397–418.

Shlain, L. (1998). *The alphabet versus the goddess: The conflict between word and image.* Viking.

Standage, T. (2005). *A history of the world in 6 glasses.* Walker & Co.

Stanton, D.C., & Stewart, A.J. (1995). *Feminisms in the academy.* University of Michigan Press.

Stronk, J.P. (2017). *Semiramis' legacy: The history of Persia according to Diodorus of Sicily.* EUP.

Voorhies, B. (2004). *Coastal collectors in the Holocene: The Chantuto people of southwest Mexico.* University Press of Florida.

Wang, J., Jiang, L., & Sun, H. (2021). Early evidence for beer drinking in a 9000-year-old platform mound in southern China. *PLoS ONE, 16*(8), 1–20.

Weber, G.W., Lukeneder, A., Harzhauser, M., Mitteroecker, P., Wurm, L., Hollaus, L.M., Kainz, S., Haack, F., Antl-Weiser, W., & Kern, A. (2022). The microstructure and the origin of the Venus from Willendorf. *Scientific Reports, 12*(1), 1–10.

Wiessner, P. (2014). Embers of society: Firelight talk among the Ju'hoansi Bushmen. *Proceedings of the National Academy of Sciences USA, 111,* 14027–14035.

Chapter Two

Desperately Wanting

Identity-Forming in Classical Civilizations circa 2000 BCE–600 CE

Classical civilizations were born when the "vague spirit of creativity" (Neville, 2019, p. 318) dawned among large communities involved in the act of "self-making . . . out of circumstances in which (they were) not fully formed" (Neville, 2019, p. 323). This creative weaving of attributes paved the way for more opportunities for people in increasingly diverse communities to come together, looking for common purpose and finding common needs.

The classical period is known for a rising population of artisans and other specialized laborers and an increase in cross-regional trade, including the Indian Ocean trade network, the establishment and development of the Silk Roads, as well as Trans-American and Trans-Saharan trade networks. This expansion of intra- and inter-regional trading practices brought with it a swell of distinct goods. It follows then that the art of the time indicates a new exploration of life, through the comfort that some found in the idea of settlement that led to new considerations and creations.

Suggestions for mindfulness aligned to this content are adapted from "Mind in a Jar" (Nhất Hạnh, 2007, p.18).

- Questions to consider: How does the story of history make me feel? How do I feel when I learn new information? How can I capture my thoughts if I am feeling overwhelmed by my reactions to information?
- How to stay in a state of mindfulness as you read: Consider that your thoughts are a vase filled with water, clear and transparent. Now imagine that you have jars of sand in front of the vase that come in a spectrum of different colors, each representing an emotion you experience. When you read, you probably experience many different emotions in response to the content you are working with. Imagine that with each emotion, that color of sand is added to the water in the vase, which causes the sand to

swirl around in the water. It will not take long for the vase of your mind to become muddled with so much sand. That sand is important. We need those emotions, but we also need stillness to be able to think clearly. From time to time, allow yourself to step away from the content and practice stillness to be able to stay in the moment, receiving the content in a way that helps your mind stay clear and calm.

GUIDING QUESTIONS

- How were arts in early classical civilizations influenced by their geography?
- How were arts of the classical civilizations indications of the relationship classical citizens had with their gods?
- How did governing systems use art in early classical civilizations?
- How were trading systems impacted by the arts in early classical civilizations?
- How did art signal the end of an empire?

The concept of place provides a space to grow this exploration both as a setting for and about the art that classical artists created. Where classical civilizations were geographically located directly impacted the art and artful expressions of a region—and that makes sense. People cannot create with materials they do not have or know about; citizens in early civilizations worked with what they had.

In Mexico, the Olmecs created art with jade and obsidian, a material found in abundance in the dormant volcano that surrounded them. Classical architecture provides a powerful window into how citizens of the time thought of their gods and into the mysteries of the past that we still are in the process of understanding. Some scholars deem the Olmec heads as evidence of a trans-Atlantic migration of Africans into the Americas while others disagree; in any event, one can agree that the Olmec heads represent "a complex interweaving of precolonial, colonial and postcolonial histories, identities and poetics" (Dudley, 2020, p. 831), as well as evidence that Olmecs were creative, resourceful, and expressive.

Among other inventions the descendants of the Olmecs, the Maya, might have adapted to using, "water pressure technology would have been useful through the display of power and knowledge, similar to how priests and shamans used astronomical events" (ANI, 2009). The ruling elite were believed to be in control of the water supply, which reinforced their power to lower-ranking citizens (Scarborough, 1998). A similar practice of using landmarks and other formations to indicate different social standings was happening farther north, with citizens of the Mississippian culture (Diaz-Granados et al., 2018). The Mississippian people spread over most of what is now the southeastern region of the United States. Their culture was centered on chieftain-based tribal diplomacy, large settlements along rivers, agriculture, complex religious and social structures, and craftsmanship (Anderson & Sassaman, 2012) that included platform mound-building (Kassabaum, 2021). This kind of innovation alludes to that spark needed to indicate that not only were Indigenous American civilizations depending on continuing certain frameworks in their society, but they were also growing into their collective identity tribally, trans-regionally, and at times, trans-continentally.

Geographic citizenship also comes into focus regarding identity building through stories. Consider places like Eurafrica, where "myth is thus inexorably connected with the Mediterranean Sea and the idea of sea travel" (Guardiola, 2017, p. 93), which sometimes included telling stories about lost places such as Atlantis. Although Atlantis might have been the birth of Greek narrative fiction (Gill, 1979), Atlantian stories might also have been an allegory, a geographic warning, a history lesson, or an expression of faith (López-Ruiz, 2022).

Greek, and later Roman religion represented a fusion of belief systems that sometimes, when combined, became something else altogether. Think about the absorption of the Assyrian goddess Atargatis and the Akkadian goddess Ishtar into Greek belief systems; this led to a single, new goddess, Aphrodite (Hayward, 2018), which is found in 2.1.

As you engage with this sculpture, think about the style of the work. Does it look like it has been influenced by Middle Eastern art? Does it appear to take a shift toward a different way of sculpting? Then look at the animal she is holding: a dove. Doves and fish were known to be symbols of Atargatis while Ishtar claimed only the dove as sacred. It is interesting to note that here Aphrodite is seen with the dove, yet her birth story has her emerging from the waves along a coastline. This weaving together of beliefs is an important indicator of not only cultural fusion, but also a changing mindset of the people who created this sculpture.

Notice the care that is given to the detail of her hair and clothing; some scholars maintain this detailing by the sculpture was a way to indicate status and respect, while other scholars think this reinforces a rising patriarchy (Kraemer, 1994). Despite Aphrodite and other goddess worship providing evidence of the sacred feminine maintaining her power during the classical era, this period is in some ways also seen as a sunset of feminine power and a shift toward patriarchal rule (Sridhar, 2021). Nevertheless, it is notable that the practices of those who worshiped Aphrodite remain mystifying as the rituals associated with such worship were kept secret.

Figure 2.1. Aphrodite, the Great Goddess of Cyprus; created c. 450-425 BCE.

Figure 2.2. Theseus Minotaur Mosaic, created c. 3rd-4th century CE.

The Cult of Mithras provides a masculine contrast to Aphrodite worshipers as well as other grounds for tangible cultural braiding. Look at figure 2.2, a mosaic of the labyrinth found in the story of the Minotaur being slain by Theseus.

However, despite this description, some scholars posit that the story told here provides another example of cultural fusion that pulls together the Persian sun god, Mithra, and the Greek demi-god, Perseus (Ulansey, 1991). Consider that there could be more to this story. Maybe the labyrinth was not really a maze at all, but rather an indication of one's thoughts, a jagged, edged way to describe what can at times feel indescribable: the act of thinking. In that regard, this mosaic illustrates a cognitive revolution of sorts, a new way of thinking about thinking. Maybe instead of being an actual creature, the minotaur was symbolic of a primitive awareness that lived inside the thoughts of those who were participating in a mindfulness practice of finding and overcoming their own inner bull.

Take a moment to reflect:

- Do you think the symbology found in the Cult of Aphrodite and the Cult of Mithras could have been created with deeper meaning, something secret that was only known to those who practiced that sort of worship?

- How could citizens publicly express devotion to a private religion?
- Do we have similar experiences in today's world? Where?
- Sit for a moment and consider these; see where your mind journey takes you and then express your ideas in a way that makes sense to you.

Australian tribespeople took the journey into cognition in a different direction with Dreaming, a belief about the interrelatedness of all humans, and all beings. Like the Cult of Mithras, this practice remains mysterious, as talking about it with outsiders is *kapu*, forbidden. Dreaming and Dream Time stories vary from tribe to tribe, yet the awareness of and belief in a common totemic ancestor (Penney et al., 2016, p. 20), a past and present closely tied to dreaming, as well as rock art like the Bradshaw rock painting, seen in figure 2.3, remain persistent between and among family groups.

Gods and godlike heroes abound in classical stories and with them, the mythos of what it takes to be a good leader. Odysseus and Penelope, for example, provide a starting point for understanding what it meant to be a good Greek, despite the complications that came about as a result of their decision-making, which was influenced by human factors that made action-taking complicated (Dobel, 2006). Stories like these provide a tool for those experiencing the tale to measure themselves against—a kind of moral-calibration method that provided examples and non-examples of what was expected, acceptable and unacceptable, inappropriate and exemplary behavior.

Figure 2.3. Bradshaw Rock Paintings, date of creation uncertain.

In India, the warrior emperor, Ashoka, provides a fascinating exploration further into human complexity with his stupas, "a visible aspect of social and scared landscapes" (Lahiri, 2015, p. 202). The ruler of a Hindu majority, Ashoka is known for being a successful warlord, who, after a particularly brutal battle, saw the carnage that he and his army had caused and upon reflection had a conversion moment, renouncing violence and converting to Buddhism. Ashoka then erected stupas throughout his territory that not only outlined his edicts, or laws, and a code for behavior, in multiple languages, but also provided little resting areas for humans and their animals. These edicts, as well as the stupas themselves, were a contributing factor to the reputation of Ashoka (Alexander, 1949), the solidity of the Silk Road trade network, and the foundation for what would become the Golden Age of India.

The Art of War is traditionally credited to Sun Tzu and is believed to have been written between 544 and 496 BCE. It is composed of thirteen chapters, each one devoted to an aspect of warfare and how it applies to military strategy and tactics. Still, there are broader strokes to the work presented in this piece, including discussions on intelligence, self-discipline, and self-awareness. This is interesting because although a definitive answer has not been reached regarding the authorship of the text, the impact of the ideas found within its words is threaded throughout the cultural tapestry of China. For example, *The Art of War* states, "The supreme art of war is to subdue the enemy without fighting," and the application of that can be found in one of the most recognizable structures of global history, as seen in figure 2.4, The Great Wall of China.

The Wall was intended to be a structure that could make a declaration without needing to engage in war. Built by Emperor Qin Shi Huang around 221 BCE, the laborers for the start of this work were made up mostly of soldiers and convicts. And even though as many as four hundred thousand people died during the Wall's construction, this was not seen as a bad omen. Instead, it was believed that the strength of the lifeforce of those who died helping build it would only serve to make the wall stronger. This evidence of architecture as art has an added component of protection, a show of power and reverence to tien, to God or Heaven. Like the dynasties of China, the construction of the Great Wall continued long after Qin Shi Huang, expanding to Yemen Pass and becoming an important garrison (Torr, 2018).

Greece provides an interesting perspective on why alliances are important but can ultimately lead to a downfall. Thucydides, an Athenian general and historian, offers a unique window into the Peloponnesian War in his writings, which he hoped would not be seen as art, as he felt Homer's works were. Instead, Thucydides wanted his writing to exist forever (trans. 1963). Still, his robust descriptions leave an artful, almost scientific impression of the war

Figure 2.4. The Great Wall of China, construction began in 3rd century BCE.

that proved to be the death toll for independent city-states, paving the way for Alexander the Great and his Hellenistic reign, his visage preserved in coinage of the time (Gatzke, 2021) a civic art, when in circulation, that could not be denied.

Cleopatra is one of the world's most intriguing leaders. "She was widely regarded, even by her detractors, as having a brilliant intellect and of being a political mastermind" (Adonis & Long, 2016, p. 53)—she knew how to build and maintain good relationships, which may have benefited her both socially and politically. Although veiled in mythos, there is evidence that she loved

Julius Caesar, and in creating an alliance with him, she made a powerful enemy of Octavius. When Caesar unknowingly left her pregnant, Cleopatra used her knowledge of the power of religious propaganda to cultivate further devotion to her and her child by ordering a statue of herself built in the image of both Venus and Isis (Roller, 2010), solidifying her status as linked with the Divine Feminine both in Rome and Egypt.

After Octavius assassinated Caesar, Cleopatra not only found that she, her child, and her country were locked in a dangerous position politically, but also that she was the subject of smear campaigns in Rome led by Octavius. In leading a coup to assassinate the previously well-liked Caesar, and in rejecting his co-members of the second triumvirate, Octavius needed positive propaganda in Rome to win over his own citizens (Yavetz, 1984). In watching this unfold across the Mediterranean, Cleopatra used her cleverness and an understanding of the power of art and religious propaganda again in her favor in crafting a barge to use as leverage to gain another powerful, necessary ally in Marc Antony. It is said that Cleopatra loaded the barge with food and women to gain the favor not only of Marc Antony, who was first a soldier and then a rejected member of the second triumvirate, but also of his men. Although the barge and much more of the story of Cleopatra is etched from myth, Plutarch (Drouet, 2022) and other contemporary historians, including Strabo, Velleius, Valerius Maximus, Pliny the Elder, Appian, Josephus, and Dio (Roller, 2010), also provide various accounts illustrating more of who she was: a powerful woman, mother, and leader who claimed and overcame.

Interactions in classical civilizations were not always hostile, and in many instances, they included examples of cooperation and community building between and among cultures in ways that archaeologists are still uncovering. In Rome, citizens sometimes co-worshiped with concurrent cultures, including the Etruscans, as is indicated by recently discovered bronze statues at a sacred thermal spring (Winfield, 2022). This was perhaps a common dovetailing cultural practice by Romans, who were known for their cosmopolitanism (Bradley, 2020).

Positive relationship building also happened through trade. As Northrup and others state (2014), "Trade has operated as more than just an economic activity; it also shaped human relations and the history of humanity" (xxv). That makes sense when one considers the action of what is happening inside of trade—one person exchanges goods or services for a good or service that is deemed as equal or more important in value. Trade hubs increased throughout the classical world and included trans-American, trans-Saharan, and other trade networks, the Silk Roads, and the start of large-scale trans-oceanic trade systems in places like the Indian Ocean.

26   *Chapter Two*

Carthage serves as an excellent example of not only economic activity, but socio-political fusions that came along with it as a facilitator of maritime trade (Bockmann, 2022). There are plentiful examples of symbiotic influences occurring between and among the Carthaginians and Greeks early on, with binding validations through artifacts and literature from works like the *Aeneid* providing connections between Greek mythos and the historical past of North Africa, even as early as 500 BCE (Grant, 1971). Seeking out connections and creating common bonds through storytelling as a preservation of things past—real or imagined—provides an important road map for cultivating shared spaces that people then occupy together, both physically and mentally.

Religion also provided an opportunity to create cultural bridges. African, specifically Ethiopian, Christianity shared a complicated history (Rukuni & Oliver, 2019) with its northwestern counterpart—Byzantium. The Ethiopian Church provides a synthesized perspective of both Judaism and Christianity (Hammerschmidt, 1965) that remained mostly isolated from the influence of outside factors such as the Council of Nicea, which convened in 325 CE. The Ethiopian kingdom of Axum not only celebrated their status as Christians and tradespeople, but they also married those ideologies in their currency, as seen in the stamped cross on the coin found in figure 2.5.

Notice that the coin is not only gold, denoting the wealth of Africa, but when found in excavation sites, these coins provide a clear artifact of extensive interregional trade networks (Beaujard, 2022) that we know shared not only artful influences, but common religious practices.

The cosmopolitan Byzantium (Pieper, 2021) provides a liminal space to embody the shifting ideologies of the time between classical civilizations and the Middle Ages. The Council of Nicea, called by Constantine in 325

Figure 2.5.   A gold coin of King Ousas from Axum, created c. 5th century.

CE, aimed to clarify a centralized belief in Christianity. Still, this process might have left some feeling unheard or unrecognized, as is illustrated in figure 2.6.

Figure 2.6. The First Council of Nicea with Ten Men and a Text of the Nicean Creed in Greek, created c. 381 CE.

Note the five men in the front; they have distinctive features and halos, while the men in the back also have halos but do not have their faces shown, despite the influence that we can infer that they also had at the meeting since they were included at all in this piece. There is a story there, some fragmented foretelling that the Church will not be as united as it seemed. And yet, Eastern Rome survived.

Western Rome fell, with sharp splinters of dissention spreading slowly. Throughout the military, for instance, loyalty grew not to Rome as was intended, but rather to individual generals. This was a crack in the system that had been present even as early as Julius Caesar in 44 BCE, and it continued to crumble along with other issues, like a lack of resources to sustain the growing population and civil unrest. Internal factors like bad rulers, and external ones like Visigoths, Huns, and others, continued to pressure the empire until Western Rome fell and ceased to exist in the fifth century (Goldsworthy, 2009), leaving shock and quiet spaces ripe for new developments.

Art and architecture were consistently used to illustrate and reinforce socio-political power, even including distinctive stratification in bathhouses and bathing practices (Perdew, 2015), which were at times seen as an extreme form of self-care. No one quite illustrates this as well as Procopius in his *Secret History* as he describes the controversial Empress Theodora:

> Her body she treated with more care than was necessary, yet less than she herself could have wished. For instance, she used to enter the bath very early and quit it very late, and after finishing her bathing, she would go thence to her breakfast . . . and though she had to such an extent strayed into every path of incontinence for so long a portion of the day, she claimed the right to administer the whole Roman Empire. (trans. 1966, p. 179)

This work has been selected by scholars as being culturally important, particularly in foundational world history or Western civilization courses. One very important detail that is often overlooked when visiting the literature is that the piece should also be considered a complicated example of what discussing politics through an expressive lens can look like (Lung, 2018), which may or may not have included affection, or even scorn, for Theodora—the Byzantine empress by Procopius, the writer who intended for his work to be published after his death.

Shifting farther west to the Mayans, affection and scorn persist even as an empire is falling. Like what occurred in Rome, the Mayan collapse included internal factors that might have meant the end of a royal line, as indicated in stelas (Driew, 1999) like the one in figure 2.7.

Desperately Wanting 29

Figure 2.7. Stela B, a high relief sculpture from Copán depicting the king Uaxaclajuun Ub'aah K'awiil; date of creation uncertain.

But why is that significant? What did the end of a dynasty imply more broadly for an entire people? This continues to be explored. But other inside issues, like a rising population and an agrarian crisis, could also have contributed to the collapse, particularly taken in tandem with the rising presence of warfare (Sheets, 2003). And with those mere words telling of the indescribable, another empire fell.

This chapter began with an invitation to mindfulness that included an adaptation of the "Mind in a Jar" activity. This suggestion was offered to help keep the mind open to the content presented, which included ways in which citizens from classical civilizations created art that was influenced by their geography, represented their reverence for the gods, and was a form of expression and asserted societal norms to their growing populace that included increased trade practices. Art was also used to indicate the fall of an empire. You will find a few ideas in table 2.1 that you can use to help you bring this into your classroom. Remember that, like the text, these activities are not prescriptive, nor are they exhaustive. Please use these to find what works best for you and for your students.

Table 2.1.

Warmup	Suggested activities	Closing
Lesson 1. Ask students, "What resources do we have readily available here in our classroom?" Have them share out and discuss. Then expand the conversation by asking, "What resources do we have that the citizens in classical civilizations also had access to?"	• Construct classical civilizations art stations for students to visit that provide visuals from the time like those found in the chapter, particularly those that contain components alluding to environmental considerations. • Assessment: Students will create a song or story to share with the class providing insight into how they feel their lives and resources today are both similar and different to those in classical civilizations.	• Exit ticket: Students will do a quick write on what they thought was the most similar resource access that they have in common with citizens in classical civilizations and why.
Lesson 2. Ask students, "Does today's art give us information about anything other than someone's freedom of expression? Where? How do you know?" Allow time for consideration and discussion.	• Choose one piece of classical art or architecture for your students to consider from four of the classical civilizations in the chapter, then walk them through the steps of the "See, Think, Wonder" strategy for one of the pieces (see Gumulya, 2022, for detailed information on how this supports tiered and supported instruction), then allow students to explore the others independently. • Assessment: Ask students to create a character who lived in one of the classical civilizations they explored and then write a journal reflecting on what they think about the art they experience in their daily lives.	• Turn and talk. Ask students whether they think citizens in classical civilizations interacted with art as much as we do today, then ask them to explain with, "Why? Why not?" Ask students to share out or do a "parking lot" post it to close.
Lesson 3. Ask students, "Do you think art influences trade in today's world? Why? Why not? How?" Allow students to share out and discuss.	• Create files with banks of information that include maps, rulers, timelines, and ideologies of the classical civilizations in this chapter. Then, using flexible grouping, ask students to become subject matter experts not only on the art of the civilization, but also to think about how the art from surrounding areas might have influenced that civilization. • Assessment: students create a visual representation (an "artifact") of the civilization they researched and share out, using movement to simulate the act of travel and trade that could have been influenced by artisans of the past.	• Quick write. Ask students to create three hashtags to represent the influence that art had on trade in classical civilizations.

References

Adonis, J., & Long, P. (2016). *How to be great: from Cleopatra to Churchill—Lessons from history's greatest leaders*. Nero.

Alexander, P.C. (1949). *Buddhism in Kerala*. Annamalai University.

Anderson, D., & Sassaman, K. (2012). Recent developments in southeastern archaeology: From colonization to complexity. Society for American Archaeology. Asian News International. (2009, December 26). Ancient Mayans may have used fountains and toilets. *Asian News International* (New Delhi, India).

Beaujard, P. (2022). Ancient connections between Asia and East Africa (1st through 15th centuries). In P. Ziltener & C. Suter (Eds.), *African-Asian relations: Past, present, future* (pp. 18–29). Wien/Zürich/Münster: Lit.

Bockmann, R. (2022). African Rome. The city of Carthage from its Roman (Re-) foundation to the end of the Byzantine period. In R.B. Hitchner (Ed.), *A Companion to North Africa in Antiquity*, pp. 117–141. John Wiley & Sons.

Bradley, G. (2020). *Early Rome to 290 BC: The beginnings of the city and the rise of the republic*. Edinburgh University Press.

Diaz-Granados, C., Simek, J., Sabo, G., & Wagner, M. (2018). *Transforming the landscape: Rock art and the Mississippian cosmos*. Oxbow Books.

Dobel, J.P. (2006). Mortal leadership in Homer's *Odyssey*. *Public Integrity, 8*(3), 215–231.

Drew, D. (1999). *The lost chronicles of the Maya kings*. Weidenfeld & Nicholson.

Drouet, P. (2022). The '(de)territorialising' power of Cleopatra's barge: Plutarch, Shakespeare, and Mankiewicz. *Cahiers Élisabéthains, 108*(1), 136–151.

Dudley, I. (2020). Olmec colossal heads in the paintings of Aubrey Williams. *Art History, 43*(4), 828–855.

Gatzke, A.F. (2021). Heracles, Alexander, and Hellenistic coinage. *Acta Classica, 64*, 98–123.

Gill, C. (1979). Plato's Atlantis story and the birth of fiction. *Philosophy and Literature, 3* (1), 64–78.

Goldsworthy, A. (2009). *How Rome fell: Death of a superpower*. Yale University Press.

Grant, M. (1971). *Roman myths (1st edition)*. Weidenfeld & Nicolson.

Guardiola, R.R. (2017). *The Ancient Mediterranean Sea in modern visual and performing arts: Sailing in troubled waters*. Bloomsbury Academic.

Gumulya, D. (2022). Developing peer tutoring digital notes with see, think, wonder thinking routine. *SENADA (Seminar Nasional Manajemen, Desain Dan Aplikasi Bisnis Teknologi), 5*, 226–236.

Hammerschmidt, E. (1965). Jewish elements in the cult of the Ethiopian Church. *Journal of Ethiopian Studies, 1*(2), 1–12.

Hayward, P. (2018). *Scaled for success: The internationalisation of the mermaid*. John Libbey Publishing.

Kassabaum, M.C. (2021). *A history of platform mound ceremonialism: Finding meaning in elevated ground* (1st ed.). University Press of Florida.

Kraemer, R.S. (1994). *Her share of the blessings: Women's religions among pagans, Jews, and Christians in the Greco-Roman world.* Oxford University Press.

López-Ruiz, C. (2022). *Not exactly Atlantis: Some lessons from Ancient Mediterranean myths.* Springer Nature Singapore.

Lung, E. (2018). Procopius of Caesarea's "History of Wars" and the expression of emotions in Early Byzantium. *Hiperboreea Journal, 5*(2), 5–24.

Neville, R.C. (2019). *Metaphysics of goodness: Harmony and form, beauty and art, obligation and personhood, flourishing and civilization.* SUNY Press.

Nhất Hạnh, T. (2007). *Planting seeds: Practicing mindfulness with children.* Parallax Press.

Northrup, C.C., Bentley, J.H., Eckes Jr., A.E., Manning, P., Pomeranz, K., & Topik, S. (2014). *Encyclopedia of world trade: From ancient times to the present: From ancient times to the present: Vol. 1* [Enhanced Credo edition]. Routledge.

Penney, B., Teague, G., & Culture Smart! (2016). *Australia—culture smart: The essential guide to customs & culture.* Kuperard.

Perdew, L. (2015). *History of art.* Essential Library.

Pieper, C. (2021). Cosmopolitanism and the Roman Empire. Political, theological and linguistic responses—Three case studies (Cicero, Augustine, Valla). *Journal of Latin Cosmopolitanism and European Literatures, 5,* 1–26.

Procopius. (1966). *The Secret History.* Penguin Books.

Roller, Duane W. (2010). *Cleopatra: A biography.* Oxford University Press,

Rukuni, R., & Oliver, E. (2019). African Ethiopia and Byzantine imperial orthodoxy: Politically influenced self-definition of Christianity. *HTS Teologiese Studies, 75*(4), 1–9.

Scarborough, V.L. (1998). Ecology and ritual: Water management and the Maya. *Latin American Antiquity, 9*(2), 135–159.

Sridhar, N. (2021). *Menstruation across cultures: The Sabarimala confusion—A historical perspective.* Global Collective Publishers.

Thucydides. (1963). *History of the Peloponnesian War.* Translated by Rex Warner, Penguin Classics.

Torr, G. (2018). *The Silk Roads: A history of the great trading routes between east and west.* Arcturus.

Ulansey, D. (1991). *The origins of the Mithraic mysteries: Cosmology and salvation in the Ancient world.* Oxford University Press.

Winfield, N. (2022). *Discovery of bronzes rewrites Italy's Etruscan-Roman history.* In AP Top News Package. Associated Press DBA Press Association.

Yavetz, Z. (1984). The res gestae and Augustus' public image. In F. Millar and E. Segal (eds). *Caesar Augustus: Seven Aspects,* pp. 1–36. Clarendon Press.

Chapter Three

Immigrant Singing

Movement and the Post-Classical Era Circa 600 CE–1500 CE

Transitions often occur when they must, born from the remnants of what remains when conditions have deteriorated the growth or development of anything else. That is where the conceptual framework of the Middle Ages is situated: there in that liminal space, between the bones of classical civilizations and the creative webbings of leftover tradition, came the spark of a new beginning, a world lit only by fire.

Suggestions for mindfulness aligned to this content are adapted from "What Am I Made Of?" (Nhất Hạnh, 2007, p. 127).

- Questions to consider: What is your day made of? What do you eat and drink? What do you wear? What music do you listen to? What do you read? What programs do you watch? What organizations are you a part of?
- Extend your thinking: Where are those components of your day from? Do they all come from one place or many different places? How did those foods and other materials or ideas make their way to you and into your daily experience? What movement of goods, services, and ideas had to happen for you to experience your day the way that you do? Keep movement in mind as you consider this content.

GUIDING QUESTIONS

- What demographic, economic, environmental, political, and social changes were expressed in art after the collapse of classical or otherwise established civilizations?
- How did movement create cultural connections in the arts?

- How did art reinforce the social, political, and economic structures of the society where they were created?
- How did art reinforce notions of empire?

Although the post-classical period in Western Europe used to be referred to commonly as the Dark Ages, one hopes that through this examination of art and culture you may find there is much more to consider. After the fall of the Roman Empire, towns collapsed due to a lack of a central governing body for support and resources, but they didn't disappear—they just fell into disrepair. This, in tandem with Viking raids, led to a new way of life for those in Western Europe and signaled a major theme from this period: outside influences directly shaping and changing the communities they encountered.

A recently discovered shipwreck in France was described by researchers as an "exceptional testimony to the naval architecture of the . . . Middle Ages," with radiocarbon dates placing the found objects as being created circa 680–720 CE (Adams, 2022); this provides an excellent foundation for this chapter's discussion. Vikings forced the chaos of Western Europe into a settled pattern of fortification built out of socio-political necessity. Their invasions were based around a need for food resources and a want for treasure, which sometimes meant women, and that shifting populace gradually came to mean a shifting culture. These sudden raids scoured waterways of England and France, causing a persistent need for restructuring that could accommodate an abrupt drain of resources like Viking raids did.

Although not all Norsemen and women went Viking, the care and attention of their villages on the materials connected with Vikings are evident in the artistry found on preserved ships such as the *Oseberg* (detail seen in figure 3.1).

Patterns such as these were common at the time throughout mainland Scandinavia (Snow, 2020) and surely held deep meanings for those constructing them as well as those sailing on ships, with the creative capital used here indicating not only that maritime travel was important in life, but that the consistency of its importance would surely follow into death.

Archaeologists and other social scientists are still determining how far the Vikings explored and settled. We know that Vikings left cultural and sometimes DNA footprints where they traveled. Recent technology has supported such findings, including the origins of the Kievan Rus, with historians like Logan stating, "in 839, the Rus were Swedes; in 1043 the Rus were Slavs" (2005, p. 184). One is left to wonder what other places will be found as home to the descendants of Vikings.

Although exploration into such matters is still in its early stages, the influence of Vikings on English history cannot be denied with cultural imprints found in art such as the epic poem *Beowulf*, which features no English

Figure 3.1. Artistic detail along the Oseberg; created in 820 CE.

characters, yet served an important enough purpose to English citizens that it was recorded. The act of recording in and of itself at the time required resource capital including vellum and other materials, and intellectual capital in the form of a literate writer to legibly write the story and its significance as historically or artistically meaningful. Again, the reasons for these creations continue to be debated today. Nevertheless, the Viking Age concluded with some scholars bringing forth the idea that when raids were occurring and women were taken back to Viking villages, eventually that practice led to a kind of cultural dissolution, with Viking children being born to Christian mothers leading Viking children to be raised with the Cross, and not Odin. This becomes abundantly clear as a Norwegian king became the first monarch to lead his men on a crusade (1107–1110), beginning a trend—kings going on crusade (Phillips, 1997)—as well as providing a subtle nod to future generations that the era of Northmen Viking raids had faded.

Earlier and elsewhere, the Golden Age of Islam (750–1150) dawned on the heels of the age of Muslim conquest that saw Arabian victories in Persia, Byzantium, North Africa, and parts of Europe, including Cordoba, which became the capital of Muslim Spain and was the most diverse city in the world for a time (Lombard, 2009). During this vibrant era, Muslim scholars explored subjects without restraint of theology or dogma, offered extremely liberal lending policies at their libraries, and provided a cohesive space for learning from different cultures, including Hellenistic, Persian, Syrian, Hindu, and other scholars (Nakosteen, 1964). These examples of scholarship might have been included in the House of Wisdom, as depicted in figure 3.2.

Cordoba, Spain, embodied the spirit of openness that the House of Wisdom centered around, because of its dedication to fairness in a diverse populace. During the time, the Mediterranean was a place of vibrant and complex identities (Horden & Purcell, 2006), and Spain was the natural intersection for many groups of people. In an effort to fairly judge those in court, particularly those from commercial operations, a consular court was set up (Register, 1918), which provided distinct judges, rulings, and at times punishments based on decisions passed down from a judge who practiced the same faith as the accused. This is one of many examples of pre-Inquisition Spanish policy that was intended to provide both justice and support to the varied cultural tapestry of citizens inhabiting Spain.

The rise of Islam meant the expanded construction of mosques. As these holy structures increased in build frequency, their architecture became influenced by the other sacred spaces, including churches. Some scholars contend that the addition of the minaret, a tower built into or next to a mosque that is used for the call to prayer, was because of the influence of the architecture in church steeples, particularly from churches in Syria (Bloom, 2013). The reciprocity that existed between Christianity and Islam is complex, and nowhere is that more evident than when one considers the impact of the crusades, which shaped the socioeconomic and cultural fabric of the Latin East in complex ways (Gutgarts, 2021). One sustaining factor throughout that

Figure 3.2. Scholars at an Abbasid library. Maqamat of al-Hariri Illustration by Yahyá al-Wasltl, created in 1237.

time of conflict was the influence of art in the Muslim world, which included the original telling of *One Thousand and One Nights*. The earliest versions of the stories were told starting around the eighth and ninth centuries and building additions to the volume through the years with contributions from India, Persia, Iraq, and Arabia (Irwin, 2004). Indeed, the crusades were a time of collective strife, and yet creative works persisted as a means to preserve, process, and find meaning.

Returning crusaders in England shared their stories of the crusades as well, which included encounters of Richard and Saladin as found in the Chertsey combat tiles (Luyster, 2022), illustrating one perspective of the relationship between the two men. These opposing leaders of the third crusade left a legacy in their respective regions that carry a certain mythos, which include stories of an unlikely friendship and mutual respect. Other stories that returning English crusaders might have heard or told included Robin Hood. Court records and folk tales indicate that his influence could have resonated throughout England, even as early as the Middle Ages, when the real Robin Hood (perhaps called Robin Hode) might have lived (Ibeji, 2011).

The courts in Heian, Japan, provided a similar opportunity for storytelling, including the exploration of the world's first novel, *The Tale of Genji*, by Lady Murasaki Shikibu (Lyons, 2011). Murasaki was born into a family of scholars and raised with an elevated social status that allowed her to study and write in Japanese and Chinese, which was unique because Japanese women were traditionally excluded from learning Chinese. It is believed that her reputation as a writer allowed her to become a member of the royal courts of Japan after her husband's death, where she wrote *The Tale of the Genji* and a collection of poems. Although her original texts have been lost, investigating those that have been preserved provides an important mirror, window, and sliding-glass door (Sims-Bishop, 1990) to the past for us to relate to today.

> From the analysis of the ideal female images in *The Tale of Genji* and the political, economic, and other factors of that time, we can see the factors that affect female social status, which plays a great role in improving female status in modern society. At the same time, the analysis of the relationship between the early mythological stories and *The Tale of Genji* and their common values may play an important role in exploring the origin of the national character of modern Japan. (Xinran, 2021, p. 970)

Mystery continues to shape some understandings of the Middle Ages. Despite the question of exactly when, determined by mythos or evidence, Medieval Western universities rose throughout the period, including the University of Paris, the University of Bologna, and Oxford University (Ruegg, 1992), as citizens in Western Europe, like their Muslim counterparts, began seeking a method of rationalization due to a rediscovery of knowledge from the past (Ruud, 2001). Classes were sometimes conducted in the manner as illustrated in figure 3.3, where one can infer that the artist is trying to capture all manner of students participating in lesson proceedings.

The preservation of stories and knowledge was supported by "those who pray," which increased with the strengthening of vassalage, the binding vow of those "those who work" and "those who fight." These concise descriptions illustrate the social component of the political and economic institution of manorialism: the system that molded Medieval Western Europe and supported the warrior kings who ruled with Christianity, specifically Roman Catholicism, providing an overarching framework for Medieval European kingdoms' socio-political ways of being.

A similar feudal system existed in Medieval Japan, with actual or perceived familial ties to samurai providing the binding needed for connections to one another and to the land. Scholars of Old Buddhism and New Buddhism

Immigrant Singing 39

Figure 3.3. A university class, Bologna; created c. mid- to late- 14th century.

supported the Kamakara shogunate (Osumi & Dobbins, 1999) that established a shogun, or warrior, ruling class. This braiding of religion and the military state is evident in statues as seen in figure 3.4, which guarded the gate of a temple.

Like the varied but prominent practices of Buddhism in Japan, Confucianism remained a consistent cultural cornerstone in China during the Song Dynasty (Li, 2022), even maintaining influence during the Mongols' rule of China (Shao et al., 2022), which stretched into the largest empire in the world at the time (Berit & Strandskogen, 2010). As the Yuan expanded, the subsequent khanates were known for the spread of both peace (Yingsheng, 2005) and increasingly safe overland and maritime trade, which dealt heavily in iron wares and porcelain (Sun, 2022) exchanges, including such goods like the dish pictured in figure 3.5, which were highly valued.

As you consider the image, note the consistent flow of the coloring, ranging from vibrant to soft, and the angles and patterns that provide movement in the image indicating the advanced craftsmanship and time required for its creation. It is notable that "artisans began in imperial China as an isolated

Figure 3.4. Kongorikishi statue from 14th century Japan.

Figure 3.5. Yuan dynasty, porcelain dish from the mid-14th century.

class, whose influence slowly grew into free-market, taxable contractors" (Barbieri-Low, 2021, p. 24). That newly gained power increased during the Yuan Dynasty solidifying an increased status and influence of the merchant class.

Elsewhere and slightly earlier throughout Oceana, the Tonga Empire was experiencing a formative age that involved not only maritime trade but also a cooperation between and among tribal lines, an alliance system that is considered by some to be an early globalization movement (Lilley, 2017).

Ceramics, pottery (see figure 3.6), and other cultural evidence indicate interactions and trade across the Lapita cultures, which later gained distinction as Melanesia, Polynesia, Micronesia, and Australia (Kaeppler, 2008). Those areas can then be subdivided into more specific tribal affiliations, each with unique languages, dialogues, and cultures that became more unique as time passed. In Polynesia, each tribe had a detailed social stratification system:

Figure 3.6. Lapita pottery, date of creation unknown.

> Relative rank within the pyramid influenced social relationships, as did gender and birth order. The arts paid allegiance to these stratified sociopolitical systems by assisting in the validation of social distinctions and interpersonal relationships. Like the social systems in which they were embedded, objects were visual symbols of prestige, power, authority, and status, and were important indicators of hierarchical order. (Kaeppler, 2008, p. 5)

Here again, art is seen to reinforce notions of power in a particular but congruent vein that is consistent throughout this period.

Farther east, the Khmer Empire rose in a correlative method, as a knitting together of multiple linguistic and ethnic groups (Frewer, 2014). This saw the dedication of Angkor Wat as a Hindu temple by its patron, King Suryavarman II, seen in figure 3.7.

After his death, Angkor Wat was ransacked and later rededicated as a Hindu-Buddhist temple. A century later, an almost-parallel ideology provided the framework for the Majapahit Empire of Southeast Asia. Although there are differing understandings of the Majapahit (Aung-Thwin, 1995), including how far the empire's sphere of influence reached (Wood, 2011), a consistency in scholarship notes the empire was vast (Crib, 2013), spanning Brunei, Indonesia, Malaysia, the Philippines, Singapore, Thailand, and

Figure 3.7. King Suryavarman II depicted in a bas-relief at Angkor Wat, early 12th century.

Timor Leste. Stories of Angkor Wat were included in Buddhist monk Mpu Prapanca's work, the *Nagarakretagama* (Malkiel-Jirmounsky, 1939), written circa 1365 (Johns, 1964), which provides a tangible cultural link between the Khmer and Majapahit.

The West African kingdoms of Ghana, Songhay, and Mali had a rich history, with common trading practices that included oral traditions and histories, mythical origin stories (De Villiers, & Hirtle, 2007), having salt as a measurement of currency (Conrad, 2010), drum signaling (Gaines, 2005), and challenge days to keep society from feeling oppressed (Conrad, 2010). Mali had distinct attributes, such as the complex dynamic between women and men in society (McKissack, 1994) and animism being the primary religious and spiritual practice prior to the massive influence and conversion to Christianity and later Islam (Skattum, 2008). Still, the ninth mansa, or king, of Mali, Mansa Musa, ruled with religious tolerance as a cornerstone in his kingdom (Berit & Strandskogen, 2010). Mansa Musa was a devout Muslim, and his *hajj*, along with its resulting social, political, and economic influences throughout the African continent, continues to be debated (Bell, 1972) and affirmed (Atalebe, 2011). Still, the art of his time provides another angle for consideration, as seen in figure 3.8.

The *Catalan Atlas*, created around 1375 and attributed to Abraham Cresques, a Jewish cartographer to the Kingdom of Aragon in northeast Spain, provides an important perspective of influence: one of a pensive Muslim king, illustrated with gold adornments. It is possible that stories of Mansa Musa were transmitted by the Maghribis, a distinct Jewish trading community with remarkable influence, evident in the span of their operations (Terpstra, 2013) and that those stories may have provided a context for the *Catalan Atlas* as it was being drafted and finalized.

Figure 3.8. Catalan Atlas, 1375, attributed to Abraham Cresques.

Unfortunately, trade does not always indicate prosperity: it can also mean the spread of unwanted things, including but certainly not limited to disease. The Black Death raged through Western Europe, Northern Africa, and Asia from roughly 1346–1353, killing what historians estimate to be a third of the world's population (Gould & Pyle, 1896). With its first definitive mark on the story of Western history imprinting in the Crimea in 1347, and two strains of the disease intensifying both the impact of, and ultimately, mortality rates (Snowden, 2019), fear and death spread and gripped citizens inter-regionally, restricting trade, communication, and growth. Norway provides an illustration of the profound impact of the Black Death. The high Middle Ages saw Norway forming a state identity (Helle, 1981), but after the Plague hit, that growth fell into decay. The population of Norway, along with its influence on the global stage, declined, with farm abandonment and contracting households (Brothen, 1996) providing a bleak, but very real perspective to close the examination of this period.

This chapter has invited mindfulness about movement. The content addressed ways that demographic, economic, environmental, political, and social changes were expressed in art after the collapse of the classical and/or otherwise established civilizations. The narrative also addressed how movement created cultural connections in the arts, and how art reinforced the social, political, and economic structures of the society where they were created, as well as ways art reinforced notions of empire. Themes of power, usefulness in art, and trade emerged throughout this work reinforcing the notions of movement and the early modern period. You can refer to table 3.1 to find suggested lessons that you can use to help you bring this into your instructional practice; please use these ideas as a foundation to inspire what works best for you and for your students.

Table 3.1.

Warmup	Suggested activities	Closing
Lesson 1. Ask students, "What do you already know about the Middle Ages?" Have them share out and discuss. Expand or enrich the conversation by asking, "What do you know about that period in another region of the world?" Allow students the time to compare their answers.	• Invite students to divide into groups, or if they choose, they may work alone. Give each group or individual a piece of art from the chapter to examine. Give them a few minutes to interact with the piece and jot down ideas. Then ask: 1. How do you feel about this art? 2. What information can you gather about the people who created the art? 3. What story do you see in this art that provides insight to the artist's life? • Assessment: Students will create skits or dances to perform for the class that shows what they understand the art to mean about life at the time; others will provide appreciation at the end of each performance.	• Exit ticket: Using scrap paper, students will jot down ONE thing they are curious about from today's lesson on the art and people of the Middle Ages; they will give this to the teacher as they leave, and the teacher will use this to inform the construction of her next lesson.
Lesson 2. Ask students, "Does art tell us how to act?" or you may choose to ask, "Does art tell us who we are?" Allow time for consideration and discussion.	• Ask students to divide into groups, or if they choose, they may work alone. • Then ask work groups/individuals to choose one of the cultures that was addressed in the chapter. Students will then use the content and art from this chapter to learn about how art defined and/or reinforced identity for people of the Middle Ages. • Assessment: Ask students to craft an infographic of how art provided identity information to people of the time.	• Headlines: Have students create a headline that expresses the main idea of what they learned today. • Extend the lesson: During the next class, post student headlines around the room and conduct an activity day with a newspaper simulation. Invite your "journalists" to choose a headline to write on and spend the day as an "editor" with each class, crafting a unique newspaper based on the headlines each class chose, then post to share with other classes.

Lesson 3.
Before class begins, choose four or five of the cultures discussed in the chapter to post outside your room on the door. Create "passports" for each culture you've chosen and a work area for each that is labeled inside your classroom. As you greet students, ask them to choose a passport before they enter the room, then direct them to find a place to sit in their chosen culture's area.

- Each group will create a commercial or a living brochure to perform for the class with specific attention to what is great about their culture, including artistic accomplishments and how they were influenced through trade.
- Assessment: students will perform for each other and provide appreciation after each performance.

- Quick draw! Ask students to create a map or visual representation of the culture they felt they needed to learn more about. Remind students to label this work before turning it in!
- Extend the lesson: consider taking the feedback and asking what areas students have remaining questions about, then grow your next lesson to address this.

References

Adams, A. (2022). Archaeologists examining "Extremely rare" 1,300-year-old ship they need to water every 30 minutes. *People.com*, n.p.
Atalebe, S. (2011, January 1). Mansa Musa, the hero. *New African, 502*, 65.
Aung-Thwin, M. (1995). The "classical" in Southeast Asia: The present in the past. *Journal of Southeast Asian Studies, 26*(1), 75–91.
Barbieri-Low, A.J. (2021). *Artisans in early imperial China.* University of Washington Press.
Bell, N.M. (1972). The age of Mansa Musa of Mali: Problems in succession and chronology. *International Journal of African Historical Studies, 5*(2), 221–234.
Berit, A., & Strandskogen, R. (2010). *Lifelines in world history: The ancient world, the medieval world, the early modern world, the modern world.* Routledge.
Bloom, J.M. (2013). *The minaret.* Edinburgh University Press.
Brothen, J.A. (1996). Population decline and plague in late Medieval Norway. *Annales de Démographie Historique*, 137–149.
Conrad, D.C. (2010). *Empires of Medieval West Africa Ghana Mali and Songhay.* Chelsea House.
Cribb, R. (2013). *Historical atlas of Indonesia.* Routledge.
De Villiers, M., & Hirtle, S. (2007). *Timbuktu: The Sahara's fabled city of gold* (1st ed.). Walker.
Frewer, T. (2014). Diversity and 'development': The challenges of education in Cambodia. In: P. Sercombe & R. Tupas (eds.), *Language, education and nation-building. Palgrave studies in minority languages and communities.* Macmillan.
Gaines, J.H. (2005). The literate voice of the drum. *International Journal of Learning, 12*(5), 103–112.
Gould G.M., & Pyle W.L. (1896). *Historic epidemics: Anomalies and curiosities of medicine.* Blacksleet River.
Gutgarts, A. (2021). Between violent outbreaks and legal disputes: The contested cityscape of Frankish Jerusalem through the prism of institutional and socioeconomic conflicts. *Journal of Medieval History, 47*(3), 332–349.
Horden, P., & Purcell, N. (2006). The Mediterranean and "the new thalassology." *American Historical Review, 111*(3), 722–740.
Ibeji, D.M. (2011, February 17). *Robin Hood and his historical context.* BBC. https://www.bbc.co.uk/history/british/middle_ages/robin_01.shtml.
Irwin, R. (2004). *The Arabian nights: A companion.* I.B. Tauris.
Johns, A.H. (1964). The role of structural organisation and myth in Javanese historiography. *Journal of Asian Studies, 24*(1), 91–99.
Kaeppler, A.L. (2008). *The Pacific arts of Polynesia and Micronesia.* OUP Oxford.
Li, L. (2022). The diversity of Confucianism in the southern Song Dynasty: A comparative study of Zhu Xi's and Zhang Shi's views on taiji and human nature. *Sungkyun Journal of East Asian Studies, 22*(1), 113–127.
Lilley, B. (2017). Globalization thinking in Austalasia and Oceania. In T. Hodos (Ed), *The Routledge handbook of archaeology and globalization* (pp. 279–282). Routledge.

Logan, F. Donald (2005). *The Vikings in history*. Taylor & Francis.

Lombard, M. (2009). *The Golden Age of Islam*. Markus Wiener Publishers.

Luyster, A. (2022). Fragmented tile, fragmented text: Richard the Lionheart on crusade and the lost Latin texts of the Chertsey Combat Tiles (c. 1250). *Digital Philology: A Journal of Medieval Cultures, 11*(1), 86–120.

Lyons, M. (2011). *Books: A living history*. Thames & Hudson.

Mckissack, P. (1994). *The royal kingdoms of Ghana Mali and Songhay life in Medieval Africa*. H. Holt.

Nakosteen, M. (1964). *History of Islamic origins of Western education, A.D. 800–1350*. University Press of Colorado.

Nhất Hạnh, T. (2007). *Planting seeds: Practicing mindfulness with children*. Parallax Press.

Osumi, K., & Dobbins, J.C. (1999). Buddhism in the Kamakura period. In J.W. Hall & J. Whitney (Eds.), *Cambridge history of Japan*. Cambridge University.

Phillips, J. (1997). Who were the first crusaders? *History Today, 47*(3), 16–22.

Register, L.B. (1918). Spanish courts. *The Yale Law Journal, 27*(6), 769–778. https://www.jstor.org/stable/786482.

Ruegg, W. (1992). The university as a European institution. In H.D. Ridder-Symoens (Ed.), *A history of the University in Europe, Vol. 1*. Cambridge University Press.

Ruud, M. (2001, August 28). *Introduction: Early 11th century Europe*. [Lecture notes]. EUH 3122 The High Middle Ages. University of West Florida.

Shao, Q., Wen, X., White, P. (2022). Design thinking under the Song and Yuan Dynasties. In: *A Brief History of Chinese Design Thought*. Springer.

Sims-Bishop, R. (1990). Mirrors, windows, and sliding glass doors. *Perspectives, 1*(3), ix xi.

Skattum, I. (2008). Mali: In defense of cultural and linguistic pluralism. In A. Simpson (Ed.) *Language and national identity in Africa*. Oxford University Press.

Snow, A.C. (2020). *Art of the Viking Age*. Smarthistory. https://smarthistory.org/viking-art/.

Snowden, F.M. (2019). *Epidemics and society: From the Black Death to the present*. New Haven, Connecticut: Yale University Press.

Sun, J. (2022). Shipwreck of the Yuan Dynasty investigated at Sandao Gang, Suizhong, Liaoning Province. In *Shipwreck archaeology in China Sea: The archaeology of Asia-Pacific navigation, vol 5*. Springer.

Terpstra, T.T. (2013). *Trading communities in the Roman world: A micro-economic and institutional perspective*. Brill.

Wood, M. (2011). Archaeology, national histories, and national borders in Southeast Asia. In J. Clad, S.M. McDonald, & B. Vaughn (Eds.), *The borderlands of Southeast Asia geopolitics, terrorism, and globalization* (pp. 23–57). Institute for National Strategic Studies, National Defense University Press.

Xinran, X. (2021). The impact of the research to *The Tale of Genji* on contemporary society: Interpretation of the two dimensions of *The Tale of Genji*. *Advances in Social Science, Education and Humanities Research, 586*, 968–970.

Yingsheng, L. (2005). War and Peace between the Yuan Dynasty and the Chaghadaid Khanate (1312–1323). In *Mongols, Turks, and Others*. Brill.

Chapter Four

In the Renaissance, My Name Is Human

Circa 1400 CE–1600 CE

The Renaissance period speaks to a time of renewal, but also a time of introspection, innovation, and outreach on the international stage. Ritual and devotion led to a period of unlikely common traits across spaces in time, including the construction of great monuments that indicated a revitalization of new ways for people to express and preserve ideas. Although many of these structures remain, there is a certain amount of evanescence in that about the same number, if not more, of those structures are now lost, and we are left to gather and make inferences about their importance based on what remains.

Suggestions for mindfulness aligned to this content are adapted from *Planting Seeds* (Nhất Hạnh, 2007, p. 83): pebble meditation.

- First: Get a pebble. If you are practicing this with your students, you may give each student one pebble, or you may choose to give them more than one. Allow yourself or your students to roll the pebble(s) around in their hands, providing yourself (themselves) an opportunity to channel their thoughts and then clear their minds.
- Find your feelings: Use the pebble as a grounding tool as you are reading or considering the content of this chapter. Take breaks to give yourself time to process what you are feeling about the content and name it. For example, you may choose to record your thoughts. Write "I feel _____ (an emotion) when I learn about/hear about/discuss _____ (a topic from the content)." You may want to explore this further by saying "because" and expanding the thought outward to provide yourself not only space to find and name the feeling, but also the opportunity to reach further into your own self-awareness.

Chapter Four

GUIDING QUESTIONS

- How did art reflect a period of recovery during the early modern period?
- How did early modern art reflect changes from earlier periods?
- How did early modern art reflect continuities from earlier periods?

Muslim education changed through the years, moving from a secular standpoint to a more rigid institution that began encouraging obedience to a stratified power system rather than scholarship. Still, the scientific processes initiated by Aristotle and preserved by early Arab-Muslim scholars continued to influence the world as Western scientists took up the torch and continued toward the world of modern science (Nakosteen, 1964). In fact, the work of many Muslim translators helped enrich Western universities, contributing to the Renaissance (Nakosteen, 1964)—a rebirth of learning, yes, but also a time of curiosity about returning to the greatness of the past through a reexamination, a revival of the classical times.

When Martin Luther nailed his 95 Theses to the door of the Castle Church at Wittenberg in 1517, he began a revolution of the mind: the Protestant Reformation (Cummings, 2002). This in turn created a different kind of movement, a social movement fighting the previously established systems of social and economic power and trying to get back to what he felt were the cornerstones of Christian teachings (Parish, 2018). He was not the first person to suggest this kind of thinking, but he was the first known person not to get executed for saying these things. His ideas continued to gain public attention, his survival providing traction for his cause. He used the printing press to spread ideas, and that might have helped him gain popularity and safety (Edwards, 2004). Luther might have been unsatisfied in how his message was received by some, and his response to revolutionists resonates in his title, *Against the robbing and murdering hordes of peasants*. Regardless of the details of this revolution of mind, the main idea was clear: Christianity again had splintered. Although the Great Schism of 1054 had certainly caused a ripple effect in the community, separating the Christian faithful into Roman Catholic and Eastern Orthodox divisions (Cross & Livingstone, 2005), the Protestant Reformation created another cleave in which practitioners relied on what Luther called "faith alone" rather than on leadership, doctrine, or dogma for salvation.

Still others in the Roman Catholic Church found themselves turning to Mary for guidance and comfort in the same way they would turn to a wife or a mother (Benckhuysen, 2019, p. 91). The *Pietà* by Michelangelo provides a pointed example of this (see figure 4.1).

It is said that if the sculpture were to become animated and Mary were to rise, it would be evident that her figure is three times the size of Jesus. Some

Figure 4.1. Pieta by Michelangelo, created 1498-1499 CE.

claim this was intentional, to demonstrate Mary's influence and power as seen through Michelangelo's perspective, while others state this is simply an issue of proportion, that Mary's figure had to be larger to accommodate the form of Jesus. In any event, Mary's image was uplifted in art and prayer, including through praying the rosary, which became a theme of the Renaissance and a religious cornerstone for the Roman Catholic faith (Black & Gravestock, 2006, p. 11), another indicator of cross-cultural interaction and influence as prayer beads were adopted from the Buddhist tradition (Blackman, 2012).

Art and prayer were being synthesized at the same time in Mesoamerica with the Popol Wuj, which used code, language, and artistic components to protect sacred ideas contained therein (Alvarado et al., 2021), preserving historic and religious traditions practiced by the Mayans and their descendants, including the K'iche' people (Christenson, 2007) and later the Aztecs (ASU,

54 Chapter Four

2002). Known for their daily human sacrifices to the sun god, Huitzilopochtli, the Aztecs maintained the practice as an act of devotion to him to keep the world from plunging into darkness (Diaz del Castillo, 2012), though sacrifices to other gods were also common, even if the justification for doing so differed. For example, sacrifices to the goddess Chicomecōātl were said to keep harvests plentiful. Blood debt rituals were part of Aztec daily lives (Keber, 2019), and coupled with the site of towering pyramids, like the one seen in figure 4.2, they were a constant reminder of the greatness and power of the gods and goddesses.

Similar monuments existed farther north in the Mississippian cultures in North America; those remaining were built almost entirely of earth and shells and are in various states of preservation due to their coastal location (Helmer et al., 2022). The sphere of influence the coastal Mississippian people maintained, particularly with those in the Midwest, continues to drive research (Mehta & Connaway, 2022). In any event, evidence indicates that North American monuments, including earthen mounds, were seen as a means of

Figure 4.2. Pyramid at Tenochtitlan, date of creation unknown.

honoring the dead, grounding the present, and providing remnants for the future (Allen, 2022, p. 337).

At the same time, the Moai were being constructed and moved about in and around Easter Island. These over nine hundred structures (Lipo et al., 2013) were built to resemble ancestors who had been deified after their death. Some are facing inward, gazing toward the center of the community, while others are facing toward the ocean, appearing as guards of their people, like those found in figure 4.3.

Figure 4.3. The Moari of Easter Island, built c. 1100-1650 CE.

The story behind the construction of the Moai may be like the often-compared Olmec heads that were built in Mexico about a thousand years earlier, in that they provide a remaining visual representation of a civilization's understanding and practice of mourning (Mason, 2013).

Remembering what has been lost, even after generations, is sometimes the mark of a cultural tradition. For example, throughout the eleventh to the mid-fifteenth centuries, the Shona people (Randles, 1981), in what would become Great Zimbabwe, boasted a centralized, walled city that suffered from what many similar and great civilizations fall to: overpopulation and a depletion of resources. However, the Concial Tower, found in figure 4.4, has been established as a World Heritage site, and as such, it continues to preserve the pre-colonial story of the Shona and the greatness that once was.

Some contemporary structures were more symbolic in nature. For example, with the rise of the Tokugawa Shogunate, Japan saw a new way forward by returning to tradition. Samurai saw a revitalization of power even with an increasing populace influenced by the outside. Uprisings of new Christian converts, as well as weariness of the opium trade and other diplomatic issues with Europeans, eventually led the daimyo to forbid any form of outside innovations, either cultural or conceptual (Frédéric, 2002) to be practiced or used in Japan. The daimyo closed Japan's doors to the outside world, isolating the country in an attempt to save its culture and its people.

In the South Pacific, in a place that came to be called "New Holland," now Australia, the Gunditjmara people were maintaining an artful approach to

Figure 4.4.   Conical Tower in Great Zimbabwe, built c. 11th-15th century.

aquaculture in an area preserved today as the Budj Bim Cultural Landscape. Still, the first European explorers in the area claimed there were no land distinctions or ownership and certainly no ties to the land by Indigenous peoples of the area. Although this deception was disputed and settled in court with the *Mabo vs. Queensland* case of 1992 (Russell, 2006), the precedent set by those first Europeans disrupted Indigenous life and changed the course of history.

Sometimes quick, incomplete decisions made in small moments can create unexpected, enduring changes. For example, Ivan the Terrible accidentally killing his son Tsarevich Ivan Ivanovich, in 1581, started a series of events known in Russia as the "time of troubles." Although the Romanov family would continue the succession of tsars in later years, the decision made by Ivan in that one single, horrible action, that occurred in the blink of a moment provides a powerful and terrible point to stop and reflect on the monumental power of a moment.

This chapter has discussed ways in which societies around the globe recovered, changed, and continued around 1400–1600 CE. The content focused on art, in particular large monuments and structures created by different civilizations for somewhat similar reasons. In table 4.1 you will find a few ideas that you can use to help bring these stories and pieces of art into your classroom. Remember that, like the text, these activities are not one-size-fits-all, and they are not the only choices for pedagogy with this kind of instruction; please use these to find inspiration to create what works best for you and your students.

Table 4.1.

Warmup	Suggested activities	Closing
Lesson 1. Ask students, "What is a monumental moment?" Have them share out and discuss. Then expand the conversation by asking, "In what ways do you think people might preserve or remember a monumental moment?"	• Ask students to create a list of FIVE monumental moments from the time period. • Divide the class into flexible groups and allow them to research ways in which the monumental moment they identified has been commemorated—how, where, and by whom. • Assessment: Students will create a living brochure about the monumental moment they researched and present it to the class.	• Exit ticket: Students will do a quick write on the similarities and differences they found in monumental moments that were presented, identifying at least three of each. • Extend the learning: Ask students, "Are all monumental moments worth remembering? Why? Why not?"
Lesson 2. Ask students, "What kinds of feelings did you experience identifying and learning about monumental moments yesterday? Were there incidents that made you react with more or less intensity?" Allow time for consideration and discussion.	• Choose one feeling that students report they are experiencing when interacting with the content. Then allow students to reflect on what they think a day in the life of a person in that time would experience (i.e., waking up, gathering drinking water, eating meals); have students create a word web to help them brainstorm. • Assessment: Ask students to create a piece of visual art or a diary entry or some other form of expression to explain why they felt the way they did and how that relates to what they imagine people of the past experienced when they lived through the event.	• Turn and talk. Ask students if they think people in the past identified and/or explored emotions they felt as much as we do today, then ask them to explain their reasoning with, "Why? Why not?" Ask students to share out or do a "parking lot" post it to close.
Lesson 3. **Social and emotional ENRICHMENT.** Ask students to identify a monumental moment in their own lives but to keep it private, journaling about it for as long as needed, but at least for ten continual minutes.	• After the writing period, ask students to take a moment to reflect on what they wrote, then invite them to consider whether they would like to share out or not. Allow time for sharing. • Assessment: Ask students to create a visual representation (an "artifact") of themselves in the monumental moment they experienced and contrast it with a historic moment from this chapter or time period.	• Closing: Ask students to research and record the steps to a mindfulness practice that they can use when they remember these monumental moments.

References

Allen, C. (2022). *Earthworks rising: Mound building in native literature and arts*. University of Minnesota Press.

Arizona State University. (29 October 2002). Ceremonial burial at moon pyramid shows Teotihuacan rulers had Mayan connection. *Science Daily*.

Benckhuysen, A.W. (2019). *The gospel according to Eve: A history of women's interpretation*. IVP Academic.

Black, C.F. & Gravestock, P. (2006). *Early modern confraternities in Europe and the Americas*. Ashgate Publishing.

Blackman, W.S. (2012). The rosary in magic and religion. *Folklore, 4*, 255–280.

Carrasco, D., & Sessions, S. (2011). *Daily life of the Aztecs*. (2nd ed.) ABC-CLIO.

Christenson, A.J. (2007). *Popol vuh: The sacred book of the Maya*. University of Oklahoma Press.

Cross, F.L., & Livingstone, E.A. (2005). Great Schism. In *The Oxford Dictionary of the Christian Church*. Oxford University Press.

Cummings, B. (2002). *The literary culture of the Reformation: Grammar and grace*. Oxford University Press.

Diaz del Castillo, B. (2012). *The true history of the conquest of New Spain*. Hackett Publishing Company, Incorporated.

Edwards, M. (2004). *Printing, propaganda, and Martin Luther*. Augsburg Fortress Publishers.

Frédéric, L. (2002). *Japan encyclopedia*, 1st edition. Belknap Press.

Helmer, M.R., Chamberlain, E.L., & Mehta, J.M. (2022). A centennial perspective on archeological research trends and contemporary needs for a vanishing Mississippi Delta. *Holocene, 0* (0), 1–11.

Keber, E.Q. (2019). Surviving conquest: Depicting Aztec deities in Sahagún's Historia. In J.F. Peterson and K. Trerraciano (Eds.), *The Florentine Codex: An encyclopedia of the Nahua world in sixteenth-century Mexico* (pp. 77–94). University of Texas Press.

Lipo, C.P., Hunt, T.L., Rapu Haoa, S. (2013). The 'walking' megalithic statues (moai) of Easter Island. *Journal of Archaeological Science, 40*(6), 2859–2866.

Mason, P. (2013). *The colossal: from Ancient Greece to Giacometti*. Reaktion Books.

Mehta, J.M., & Connaway, J.M. (2022). Mississippian culture and Cahokian identities as considered through household archaeology at Carson, a monumental center in North Mississippi. In: Baltus, M.R., Baires, S.E., Malouchos, E.W., Mehta, J.M. (Eds.), *Cahokian dispersions*. Springer.

Nakosteen, M. (1964). *History of Islamic origins of Western education, A.D. 800–1350*. University Press of Colorado.

Nhất Hạnh, T. (2007). *Planting seeds: Practicing mindfulness with children*. Parallax Press.

Parish, H.L. (2018). *A short history of the Reformation*. I.B. Tauris.

Randles, W.G.L. (1981). *The empire of Monomotapa: From the fifteenth to the nineteenth century*. Mambo Press.

Russell, P. (2006). *Recognizing Aboriginal title: The Mabo case and Indigenous resistance to English-settler colonialism*, 1st edition. University of Toronto Press.
Sheiko, K. & Brown, S. (2014). *History as therapy: Alternative history and nationalist imaginings in Russia*. Ibidem.
Torr, G. (2018). *The Silk Roads: A history of the great trading routes between East and West*. Arcturus.

Chapter Five

The Beginning Is the End Is the Beginning

Colonization and Empire Circa 1450 CE–1750 CE

Global citizens continued to interact with one another in different ways. Sometimes cross-cultural contact led to meaningful changes that benefited both sides of the interaction; at other times, exposure to each other led to disaster. Destruction, reconstruction, and repurposing of tradition provide themes of the time, and of the chapter.

Suggestions for mindfulness aligned to this content are adapted from "Drawing interbeing" (Nhất Hạnh, 2007, p. 150).

- Invite students to imagine, draw, or paint something they eat or wear regularly.
- Next, ask students to brainstorm all the *people* who contribute to the production of that food or clothing. Ask students to brainstorm all the *places* that contribute to the production of that food or clothing.
- Finally, invite students to consider if the means of production that are being practiced are from an earlier tradition or if the production process is a web of activities that contains both "old" and "new" components.

GUIDING QUESTIONS

- What did exploration mean to various communities in the early modern period and how was that expressed through the arts?
- What impact did societal revolutions have on arts in the early modern period?
- How did inquiry, discovery, and acts of rebellion change or embody the arts?

As a Muslim eunuch in Ming China, Zheng He spent much of his young life enslaved. Through years of service, He eventually gained the trust of the emperor, and from then on he lived his life in a liminal, but privileged space as an admiral, explorer, and diplomat. His voyages were justified as ways to find new partnerships and tributes to China. Junks, the giant ships built to facilitate his trips, were said to be four stories tall and much larger than any other contemporary wooden ships, as indicated in the woodcut pictured in figure 5.1.

Figure 5.1. Chinese woodblock print representing Zheng He's ships, created early 17th century.

Through new connections and revitalized relationships, the Ming Dynasty experienced a fresh kind of validation from the outside. He contributed to this through his expeditions; evidence indicates his explorations might have included trips to the Americas (Menzies, 2004).

Robust curiosity and a desire for hegemony was also embodied by the rule of Queen Elizabeth I. Bound by the expectations of the court regarding her gender, a council comprised of officials from the Church and political advisors complained that she needed to marry, because, as a woman, that was her duty in order for her "to become a true woman of God." In an act of defiance or compliance, she slid a ring on her "wedding ring finger" and held it up to them, declaring that she was already married to England (Heisch, 1980). In this fleeting moment, Elizabeth used the symbol provided by the ring not only to solidify her status as a "true woman of God," but also to declare to the people of England that she considered her relationship with them as sacred as the one she could have had with a husband. As a ruler, she was still seen first as a woman, but through cleverness and symbology, she was able to maintain her status as both single and an active, ruling leader without having to compromise her feelings of self to fit the mold of societal expectations. Those binding ideologies did not limit Elizabeth. She used her power in innovative ways, connecting with the peasantry and the military (Leicester & Christy, 1919), through the arts (Beauclerk, 2010) and through piracy (Kelsey, 1998).

Sir Francis Drake, Vasco de Gama, and others began a legacy of acquisition along known and unknown seas. There were many reasons for this shift, an active scramble—one of many—to conquer, possess, and retain new lands and at times, to vie for dominance of the seas. One justification for exploration came from stories of Prester John that had been told to, and later by, crusaders. It was said that Prester John was an isolated Christian ruler whose kingdom was situated among Muslim and East Asian territories (Delaney, 2012) and that God had bestowed upon him both the Fountain of Youth and a magic mirror that could see anything in the world (Taylor, 2014). The story of Prester John was so widespread that the legend took on a life of its own, with different ideas about where and who Prester John might be. Some believed him to live in Ethiopia, as illustrated by Diogo Homem (see figure 5.2).

Others believed that Prestor John ruled one of the "three Indias," while still others believed him to be located somewhere near the Mongol horde. As time moved forward, the legend continued, and the search for Prester John and his treasures gained traction. Ponce de Leon claimed to have found the Fountain of Youth in Florida (Olschki, 1941). These fantastical treasures were being sought out even as new navigational tools were being developed. This dichotomy of movement forward in science while reaching for a mythical past further illustrates the transitional nature of this time. Thoughts and

Figure 5.2. East Africa with Prester John enthroned by Diogo Homem, created c. 1555–1559.

scholarship vacillated from ideas framed around magic toward innovation based on "new" concepts of science.

This ideological shift indicates a time marked by difficulty in finding distinction in many places, including identity building. One might ask, "Who is an explorer, and who is a pirate?" Then, "Who is a privateer? Where are allegiances, and how hearty are they in the face of controversy or diplomacy?" These are not easy questions, and they do not have easy answers. For example, Hernan Cortes, a Spanish explorer, was said to have burned his ships upon arriving in Mexico to prevent his men from retreating in battle against the Aztecs (see figure 5.3).

Figure 5.3. Hernan Cortes scuttling his fleet off the Veracruz coast, attributed to Miguel Gonzalez, date of creation unknown.

A man of the Spanish court, Cortes was known to create alliances, including with Indigenous tribespeople, that then led to solidified relationships, but sometimes also to destruction. Contact between Natives and conquistadors frequently led to disaster, including subsequent disease and genocide, and new ways of thinking through conversions to Christianity (Frank, 1989). These perhaps even led to new developments in perceptions of Christ through revolutionary iconography, including the rise of the Sacred Heart symbol (Kilroy-Ewbank, 2018), an indication of a significant cultural reciprocity on both sides of that interaction.

Cultural exchange was not a one-way street, and it certainly did not notate a fixedness for Native populations that were in the process of being "discovered" by European counterparts. "For Indigenous people, *place* was anywhere and everywhere" (Godwin et al., 2022, p. 14), including along the seas (Woodward, 2015). Yes, before, during, and after the Golden Age of Piracy, some tribespeople became pirates. Choosing a life of piracy made sense for those Indigenous people who chose to join crews because of the democratic nature (Leeson, 2009) of the ship and the culture of egalitarianism, particularly for people of color (Kinkor, 2001). This was not unlike the democratic, egalitarian systems that many Indigenous people were raised in, as democratic, egalitarian systems were a common form of tribal politics. Life aboard a pirate ship "caused the creation of social environments that were significantly more tolerant and progressive than what would have been experienced on land" (Cheng, 2017, p. 4), particularly once European settlers came, and that provided a unique and empowering opportunity that many saw and seized.

Others were not so lucky. The use of coercive and semi-coercive labor in the New World rose quickly with Indigenous populations originally targeted for that kind of work. However, death due to disease (Cook, 1998) and other factors brought forth by the colonists made Indigenous coercive labor less appealing than the prospect of the trans-Atlantic slave trade for Portuguese and other European merchants. This led to a new kind of economy and, with it, a power dynamic that is still being examined for its human cost as well as its contribution to tropical economies and power dynamics in early modern Europe, among other impacts (Fatah-Black, & van Rossum, 2015). "Slavery has been a universal human institution and remains widespread, but Atlantic slavery holds an unusual importance for thinking about modernity, foreshadowing as it did racial consciousness and industrialization of global economies" (Green, 2012, p. 4); the trans-Atlantic slave trade marked a pivot point not only in the previous practices of slavery, but also in global history. "There is little question that this forced migration was one of the great crimes against humanity in world history, which was made no better by the fact that Africans as well as Europeans participated in its rewards" (Klein & Vinson, 2007, p. 599), resulting in quickly changing family and other cultural dynamics. The stories of those Africans lost or otherwise changed along the Middle Passage have been memorialized in resistance works (Taher, 2016) and "intangible cultural heritage, as evidenced through links with religion, cultural traditions, art, and literature" (Turner et al., 2020, p. 1).

Rebellion coupled with the open sea provided some European women with opportunity, and sometimes freedom. For example, Englishwoman Mary Read grew up dressed as a boy so she and her mother could pretend she was her dead brother and continue receiving funds from her paternal grandmother, a ruse that allowed Mary to eventually join a pirate crew as a man (Cordingly, 1996). Likewise, Irishwoman Anne Bonny was born into an elaborate situation, with her mother being the servant of her married-to-someone-else father. Anne's identity was hidden as a child; she was raised as a boy by her father as a ward so they could continue getting money from his wife. Nevertheless, the scheme was uncovered, and the money flow halted; then Anne and her parents left together for North Carolina (Druett, 2001). Anne married a small-time pirate of whom her father disapproved (Lorimer & Synarski, 2002), and they moved to the Republic of Pirates, where he started working as an informant to the governor, an occupation of which Anne disapproved (Woodward, 2015), but that is also where she met Calico "Jack" Rackman, whom she took as a lover. Anne joined Rackman's crew along with Mary, but scholars are still unsure whether or how their sex and/or gender was concealed

(O'Driscoll, 2012), despite Anne having a child with Rackman who was left in Cuba (Johnson, 1724). These notions provide countless other dimensions for exploration for historically curious minds. For now, this story ends with Rackman being executed for piracy, Mary dying of fever while pregnant and imprisoned, and Anne's still-unsolved disappearance. Rackman is infamous for two reasons: having both Read and Bonny onboard his ship and being associated with flying the Jolly Roger (Konstam, 2002, p. 98), perhaps the most-recognizable symbol of the Golden Age of Piracy.

Symbols and their meanings can sometimes evolve into something new, indicating both an ending and a continuity. Religious syncretism, that is the blending of two or more religions to form a new religion, became a form of cultural preservation—but it can also be viewed as a rebellion (Dwyer, 2017). In some ways, this return to tradition, or the maintaining of it by weaving together new ideas, is a common theme throughout this period, not only in Latin America with the rise of voodoo and Santeria, and the maintaining of the autochthonous in the Andes (Sarmiento & Hitchner, 2017), but also in the Himalayas with the continuity of spiritual encounters with yetis, an experience rooted in the religion and tradition of the Lepcha and Tibetan people (Capper, 2012). These practices of maintaining or growing religious ideologies remained rooted, strengthening into a kind of cultural art that is sometimes difficult to articulate for those outside the practice.

In many parts of the world, including Europe, religious symbology included structures like churches, but metaphysical symbols as well (Tillich, 1958)—for example, the keeping of time. Although we do not know when the ringing of the bells began to be used by churches to mark the time (Walters, 1908), we do know that with the rise of mercantilism, tangible shifts occurred not only with a rising interest in time, but also with an interest in space, including the study of planetary bodies and orbits. Western theoretical explorations of space went, in many ways, hand in hand with the clockmaking revolution of the mid- to late-sixteenth century. European and Ottoman inventors (Campbell, 2006) among others experimented with creating alarm clocks to sound at a specific time based on peg placements on a dial wheel. German inventor Philipp Hainhofer is attributed with writing the first-known descriptions of a modern cuckoo clock in 1620 (Graf, 2006); a similar clock is illustrated in figure 5.4.

Ottoman inventor Meshur Sheyh Dede created a pocket watch in 1702 that marked both hours and minutes and was intricately designed to also mark the Gregorian and Arabic calendars, as well as indicate the signs of the Zodiac (Horton, 1977). These inventions indicate that not only was time being marked, with considerations for celestial bodies and multicultural awareness, but it was important to have the opportunity to provide an artistic flair to the

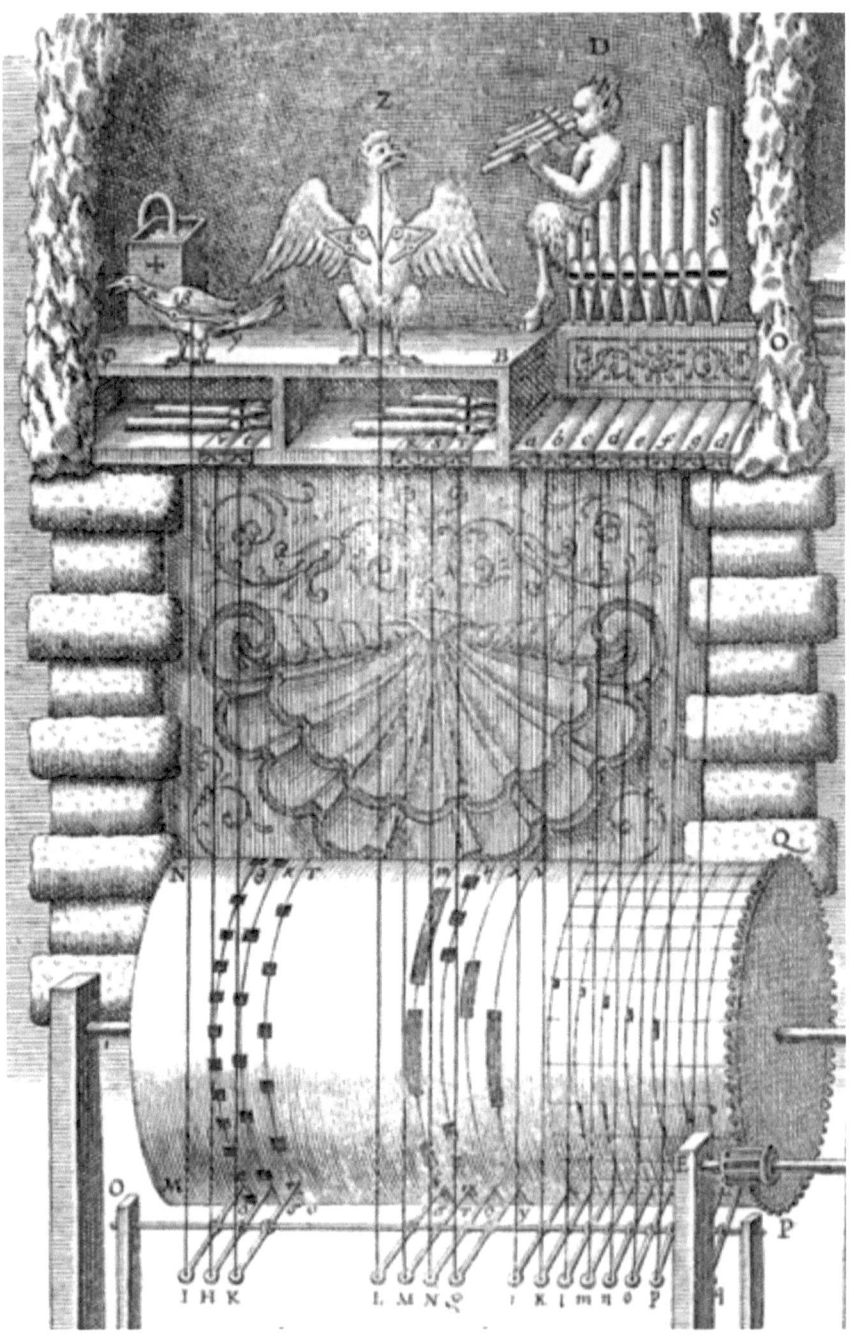

Figure 5.4. Illustration of a mechanical cuckoo clock.

status of knowing an exact time across socio-political borders. Acknowledging both time and space in such a way became another component of showing wealth and celebrating culture.

Still, nature provided another dimension to the marking of time. For example, along the Maritime Silk Roads, days and minutes became particularly delicate during certain times like monsoon season, when port cities flourished due to sailors' dependence on the winds (Torr, 2018). Still, sailors were not the only explorers on the seas; the practice of piracy remained and extended even into the Indian Ocean. There, Henry Every and his crew impacted not only their own fates, but also the treasure of the Mughal emperor, Aurangzeb, and the women they encountered onboard as they interrupted a Muslim convoy heading home from Mecca, which led to what some historians call the first global manhunt (Johnson, 2020). While some details of that interplay remain vague, the subsequent legend—coupled with the profound influence that Every's raid had at the time—was felt not only in recuperating diplomatic relations between Great Britain and the Mughal empire, but also in providing fertile ground for a strengthening of relations with both the British East India Company (Baer, 2005) and the Dutch East India Company. Here, a very real encounter brought about fear and anger. These real human responses and authentic political reactions provide a place to pause to consider, another moment to seek the humanity of others in the past. The largest part of what remains of this story is the framework of the truth, emboldened by storytelling.

In a similar vein, many contemporary women across Europe, including those who practiced any form of science, and in some cases women who were merely poor (Goodare, 1998) or were guilty only of being women, were accused of witchcraft and executed. There were social reasons for this, including religious upheaval and anti-sexual reformism (Klaits, 1985). There were political reasons for witch hunts, including new systems of ruling (Goodare, 1998). Finally, there were economic reasons for the witch hunts, too, which included bizarre correlations between weather anomalies, accusations, and executions (Leeson & Russ, 2017). The European witch hunts that ebbed and flowed between 1450 and 1750 were a complicated response to complex circumstances, and yet:

> the thread that runs through it, the only constant, is the gender of the victims. It is from the beginning, and becomes even more emphatically, a persecution of women, which sheds light on the history of persecution, criminality, poverty, religious teaching, the family, and how men and women relate to each other. (Barstow, 1988, p. 19)

Here, violence against women provides a stark framework, a continuity that shades progress of the period, even as forward movement abounds in other ways. Still, what is left in the standards-based content of the witch hunts remains sadly ambiguous, if not overlooked altogether in school curricula, eclipsed by the literary works and study of *The Crucible* or even *The Scarlet Letter*. By ignoring this rash of real-life injustice, a sense of fantastical curiosity settles rather than an invitation to uncover and subsequently prevent tragedies like this from ever happening again.

This chapter has discussed ways in which global citizens living between 1450 and 1750 changed and continued ideas and practices that came before them. Traditions provided a holding point for those clinging to the past to rebel against oppressors. New ways of thought and ways of life also provided a different angle to form new traditions that reflected new ways of being. There are draft lessons in table 5.1 that can help guide you in your pedagogy as you explore ways to bring these stories to life in your classroom.

Table 5.1.

Warmup	Suggested activities	Closing
Lesson 1. Ask students, "What are some resources we use often here in our classroom?" Have them share out and discuss. Then expand the conversation by asking, "What would you say is the resource we use most in our classroom together? What about independently?"	• Ask a student to sketch the item the class uses the most together on the board, then brainstorm the components that go into the production of that resource. For example, if the class uses pencils the most, the pencils are made of wood, wood is from trees, trees need sunlight and water, etc. • Assessment: Ask students to take those same materials needed for the resource used in the classroom and find a congruent resource used in the period. What resource is it? Was it easily accessible? How was it used?	• Exit ticket: Students will do a quick write on what they think the significance is in finding similar resources . . . how does that connect us to the past?
Lesson 2. Ask students, "What kinds of art do we see that we use?" Allow time for consideration and discussion.	• Choose one piece of art or architecture for your students to consider from the regions and content of the chapter, then walk students through the steps of the "See, Think, Wonder" strategy for one of the pieces (see Gumulya, 2022, for detailed information and how this supports tiered instruction), then allow students to explore the others independently. • Assessment: Ask students to create a piece of art that could have been used in the period using only materials that would be accessible to those of the time.	• Journaling: The students will write a journal reflecting on utility art they experience in their daily lives.
Lesson 3. Ask students, "Do you think art is a way for people to show rebellion or support in today's world? Why? Why not? How?" Allow students to share out and discuss.	• Create files with banks of information that include maps with trade routes, timelines, and ideologies of the ruling classes found in this chapter. Then, using flexible grouping, ask students to become subject matter experts, not only on the art of one of the regions, but also in thinking about how the art from the time might have shown support or rebellion.	• Parking lot. Ask students to create a piece of art that shows support of or rebellion against an idea, event, or person from the period. Have students post their work together as they exit the class • Extend the learning: Use these artifacts as talking points to begin the next lesson.

References

Baer, J.H. (2005). *Pirates of the British Isles*. Tempus Publishing.
Barstow, A.L. (1988). On studying witchcraft as women's history: A historiography of the European witch persecutions. *Journal of Feminist Studies in Religion, 4*(2), 7–19.
Beauclerk, C. (2010). *Shakespeare's lost kingdom: The true history of Shakespeare and Elizabeth*, first edition. Grove Press.
Campbell, G. (2006). *The Grove encyclopedia of decorative arts*, vol. 1. Oxford University Press.
Capper, D. (2012). The friendly Yeti. *Journal for the Study of Religion Nature & Culture, 6*(1), 71–87.
Cheng, D. (2017). Liberty in piracy. *Journal of Undergraduate Studies, 5*(1), 1–4.
Cook, N. D. (1998). *Born to die: Disease and New World conquest*. Cambridge University Press.
Cordingly, D. (1996). *Under the black flag: The romance and the reality of life among the pirates*. Random House.
Delaney, C. (2012). *Columbus and the quest for Jerusalem: How religion drove the voyages that led to America*. Free Press.
Druett, J. (2001). *She captains: Heroines and hellions of the sea*. Simon & Schuster.
Dwyer, C. (2017). The construction of the African slave identity: Defying hegemony through syncretic religious practices. *Denison Journal of Religion, 16*(7), 45–54.
Fatah-Black, K., & van Rossum, M. (2015). Beyond profitability: The Dutch transatlantic slave trade and its economic impact. *Slavery & Abolition, 36*(1), 63–83.
Frank, R. (1989). The Codex Cortés: Inscribing the conquest of Mexico. *Dispositio, 14*(36/38), 187–211.
Godwin, A.J., Abela, J. & Rice, K. (2022). Empowering Indigenous identity through instructional frameworks. *DKG: Bulletin, 89*(1), 13–23.
Goodare, J. (1998). Women and the witch-hunt in Scotland. *Social History, 23*(3), 288–308.
Graf, J. (2006). The Black Forest Cuckoo Clock: A success story. *National Association of Watch and Clock Collectors Bulletin, 48*(6), 646–52.
Green, T. (2012). *The rise of the trans-Atlantic slave trade in western Africa, 1300–1589*. Cambridge University Press.
Heisch, A. (1980). Queen Elizabeth I and the persistence of patriarchy. *Feminist Review, 4*, 45–56.
Horton, P. (1977). Topkapi's Turkish timepieces. *Saudi Aramco World, 28*(4), 10–13.
Johnson, C. (1724). *A general history of the robberies and murders of the most notorious pyrates*. Charles Rivington.
Johnson, S. (2020). *Enemy of all mankind: A true story of piracy, power, and history's first global manhunt*. Riverhead Books.
Kelsey, H. (1998). *Sir Francis Drake: The Queen's pirate*. Yale University Press.
Kilroy-Ewbank, L.G. (2018). *Holy organ or unholy idol?: The sacred heart in the art, religion, and politics of New Spain*. Brill.

Kinkor, K.J. (2001). Black men under the black flag. In C. R. Pennell (Ed.), *Bandits at Sea: A Pirates Reader*, pp. 195–210. New York University Press.

Klaits, J. (1985). *Servants of Satan: The age of the witch hunts*. Indiana University Press.

Klein, H.S., & Vinson, B., III. (2007). *African slavery in Latin America and the Caribbean* (Second edition). Oxford University Press.

Konstam, A. (2002). *The history of pirates*. Lyons Press.

Leeson, P.T. (2009). The calculus of piratical consent: The myth of the myth of social contract. *Public Choice, 139*(3/4), 443–459.

Leeson, P.T., & Russ, J.W. (2017). Witch trials. *Economic Journal, 128*(613), 2066–2105.

Leicester, R., & Christy, M. (1919). Queen Elizabeth's visit to Tilbury in 1588. *English Historical Review, 34*(133), 43–61.

Lorimer, S., & Synarski, S. (2002). *Booty: Girl pirates on the high seas*. Chronicle Books.

Menzies, G. (2004). *1421: The year China discovered America* (1st Perennial ed.). Perennial.

Nhat Hanh, T. (2007). *Planting seeds: Practicing mindfulness with children*. Parallax Press.

O'Driscoll, S. (2012). The pirate's breasts: Criminal women and the meanings of the body. *The Eighteenth Century, 53*(3), 357–379.

Olschki, L. (1941). Ponce de León's Fountain of Youth: History of a geographical myth. *Hispanic American Historical Review, 21*(3), 361–385.

Sarmiento, F., & Hitchner, S. (2017). *Indigeneity and the sacred: Indigenous revival and the conservation of sacred natural sites in the Americas*, first edition. Berghahn Books.

Taher, F. (2016). The culture of exile and narratives of resistance: A study of Munif's cities of salt and Naipaul's the Middle Passage. *Review of European Studies, 8*(3), 56–71.

Taylor, C. (2014). Global circulation as Christian enclosure: Legend, empire, and the nomadic Prester John. *Literature Compass, 11*(7), 445–459.

Tillich, P. (1958). The religious symbol. *Daedalus, 87*(3), 3–21.

Turner, P.J., Cannon, S., DeLand, S., Delgado, J.P., Eltis, D., Halpin, P.N., Kanu, M.I., Sussman, C.S., Varmer, O., & Van Dover, C.L. (2020). Memorializing the Middle Passage on the Atlantic seabed in areas beyond national jurisdiction. *Marine Policy, 122*, 1–4.

Walters, H.B. (1908). *Church bells*. A.R. Mowbray & Co.

Woodward, C. (2015). *The republic of pirates: Being the true and surprising story of the Caribbean pirates and the man who brought them down*. Houghton Mifflin Harcourt.

Chapter Six

Raging Against the Machine

Industrial and Democratic Revolutions Circa 1750 CE–1900 CE

In many ways, this chapter is the forceful embodiment of the start of Hegel's dialectic, consisting of a thesis and its correlating, but not complete, antithesis, which push against each other until a synthesis is formed, and that is where we move forward in our story. The push-pull factors of machine work, the ailments of suffering citizens, and systems of oppression evolving to a chokehold all provide a foundation for this period. And yet . . . and yet, there is art. There are people at the center of this story and with that a messiness of humanity that can never quite reach equilibrium.

Suggestions for mindfulness aligned to this content are adapted from "Breathing Meditation" (Nhất Hạnh, 2001, p. 95).

- An inquiry to pose to your students: Do you notice when you breathe? Invite students to take a moment to be aware of and connect to their breath.
- Now invite them to look around their current environment or to consider their day—what do you see here that you make use of that you are not aware of? The air-conditioning or heat? What about the chair in which they are sitting?
- Provide time for students' mindful reflection on one or more of these components of life that they may not have considered in the past.

GUIDING QUESTIONS

- How did artists use art to reinforce their ideals of revolution?
- How were human responses to revolution expressed in art?
- Why is it important for students to identify human responses in art?

The Industrial Revolution initiated quick and sustaining changes to the way life was conducted in Western Europe and beyond (Stearns, 2021). Cottage industry, homes, transportation, communication, even infant mortality and fertility rates, transitioned in quick order as technological development, the formation and refinement of states (Mohajan, 2019), and sometimes even regions, rushed to stay ahead of one another. The advent of factories went hand in hand with the rise of new kinds of work and workers, along with a new middle class consisting of bankers, investors, merchants, and others who were now replacing the previously powerful nobility (Mohajan, 2019). People flocked toward jobs in cities, particularly in England, where both circumstance and initiatives drove people from their home life and sometimes into jobs they had not picked for themselves. Factories and the work required to run them was unlike anything workers had experienced before. A breakdown of personal and hereditary ties to the land and to each other, little space or time to work in, and the tearing apart of relationships between families and neighbors led to frustration and rebellion. These were human responses to the changes brought about by the machine (Merchant, 2023). This watershed moment of new frustration is expressed in art reflecting the Luddite movement, like that seen in figure 6.1.

As you can see, the figure of Ned Ludd, the leader of the Luddites, is drawn as larger than life but not without hardship; he is missing a shoe and sports a look of exasperation. After all, there is little to no rest for the weary when one has the role of a modern-day Robin Hood, destroying new machinery that takes away the humanity and livelihood from fellow workers, a futile but noble struggle to take action when it seems there is nothing else left to be done.

Citizens of England, France, Germany, and later beyond that had much to protest. Alternative solutions to capitalism began to rise, including the idea of Marxism. Theorists grappled with which solution might last the longest. Some thought that over time, capitalism would cannibalize itself, leaving an exhausted, inhumane populace grappling for a place in the world to find resources and comfort, while others found the inverse to be true, with the theory that communism would be sustained until it eventually dissolved into underground, and then blatant runaway capitalism.

Across the Atlantic, a new kind of rebellion was taking place. Although only about a third of the population of the colonies were in support of separation, the American Revolution pushed forward under the leadership of the Founding Fathers. Complicated ideologies began to be explored, such as the formation of a democratic republic and freedom of speech. After all, freedom of speech is easy as long as everyone agrees with each other. When people disagree, freedom of speech becomes complex, a challenge that necessitates

Figure 6.1. The leader of the Luddites.

the preservation of democratic mindsets with willing, reciprocal participants. The founding of such a place is sure to provide some kinds of almost mythological origin stories, such as that told by the painting in figure 6.2.

Figure 6.2. Washington Crossing the Delaware.

As you can see in this fantastical work, there are not only many representations of citizens; this diverse makeup may be perceived to be reflective of all the kinds of people living in the colonies that would become the United States. Again, there is an air of mythos in this depiction. Consider the presence of animals, the setting, the weather . . . is there a woman included in this painting? And if so, is that significant? Why? Why not? How could that representation embody rebellion against the perceived norms of the time? What if our perception of the time is different from what life was like then? Is that possible? Why? Why not?

The French Revolution went to philosophical places in ways that many revolutions have not with the Third Estate and the salon providing pipelines for cohesion between and among populations that were tired of hunger and ripe for change. Unlike England, France did not have the economic fortitude to support rapid industry, nor did it have the financial support to feed an ailing population in the midst of famine. However, France did have an Austrian queen who was in and then out of favor with her people, which provided a place to blame and a hope for reordering society. Consider the artwork found in figure 6.3.

In this figure, you see a French peasant woman from the Third Estate nursing her child on the back of a wealthy woman, a member of the First Estate, as she leans on a nun, a member of the Second Estate. The caption reads, "*Vive le roi, vive la nation. J'savois ben qu'jaurions not tour*," meaning, "Long live the king, long live the nation. I knew well that I would not turn." This ironic statement again provides a twisted hope in its words, a perspective on change

Figure 6.3. Vive le roi, vive la nation J'savois ben qu'jaurions not tour.

knowing that progress takes time and hoping that one day power would lie with the people, and not the traditional authority of France.

After the dust had settled, but not far from the conclusion of the French Revolution, came a new power: Napoleon Bonaparte. In some ways Napoleon embodied this desire to move forward from old to new systems of authority. Napoleon's impact on the global theater is notable. Not only did he rise from a family of Corsican minor nobles, but he also fell in love with a Swedish princess and later Joséphine de Beauharnais. Napoleon reconciled France with the Church, created a public schooling system, established a public bank of France, and set forth a standard set of laws—the Napoleonic Code.

However, the pride that gave Napoleon an edge in his role as a general had a spectrum of impacts: positive, negative, and varying degrees of both. News of Napoleon's march across Europe led to subsequent revolutions, including one in Haiti, a French colony. Toussaint L'Overture led legions of Haitian former slaves in a successful revolt. News of his success was suppressed in the United States to deter others from being inspired, particularly since he and his men successfully founded the second independent nation in the New World (Baur, 1970). Still, L'Overture's story resonated. After all, under L'Overture, Haiti became a successful trade partner with the United States, Great Britain, and others. Despite being a respected diplomat, and despite attempting to maintain a positive relationship with Napoleon, L'Overture was eventually arrested by French troops who had been ordered to restore order and French rule in Haiti (James, 1814); he died in a French prison cell, where his requests for firewood, and for medical treatment, were ignored. Throughout that transitional time—the time of empowerment and then a restoration of previous power—the people of Haiti remained connected to the past through traditions such as voodoo and zombieism (Hoermann, 2017), yet the struggle began for a new identity—another hallmark of the period.

Meanwhile, Napoleon's pursuit of power also impacted the Middle East. His influence on Egypt and the broader Muslim population of Arabia created an imbalance between the Mamluks, Ottomans, and others (Bell, 2021). Some artwork depicting these incidents indicate Napoleon as a hero overcoming a divided populace, as seen in figure 6.4.

Here the artist pictures Napoleon and the French troops on large and powerful horses with organized dress uniforms and weapons, while others at the Battle of the Pyramids are depicted nude, desperately reaching toward the French. This ideology illustrates the kind of white-savior trope found in many pieces of art at the time. When Napoleon abandoned his push into the Middle East, the cultural disarray presented by him and his men created an unfortunate lasting impression, a distrust for Westerners and of each other, that persisted in Middle Eastern populations moving forward.

Still, Napoleon's influence continued. In the wake of annoyance with populations that refused to concede, he chose to sell France's holdings in North America. The Louisiana Purchase overlooked Indigenous rights to the land, but it nearly doubled the size of the United States and manifested a diverse territory, including ports, farmlands, and other geographic tapestries. As seen in figure 6.5, finalized documents transferring the Louisiana Territories from

Figure 6.4. Napoleon at the battle of the pyramids, July 21, 1798.

Figure 6.5. Hoisting of American Colors over Louisiana.

France to the United States took place in the Cabildo, the seat of the Spanish colonial city hall found in the traditionally French city of New Orleans, Lousiana.

The diversity found in New Orleans was similar in many ways to the diversity found in Latin America, where the stratified encomienda system pitted peninsulares, mestizos, and Natives against one another and their colonial originators in Spain and Portugal. Father Hidalgo and later Simon Bolivar led Latin American wars of independence that echoed similar kinds of forward democratic movement in that they liberated Mexico, Venezuela, Ecuador, Colombia, and Peru. However, freedom was not enough—more work needed to be done to create stability in the former colonies, and emancipation was never easy.

Some found creative ways to rebel against oppressors. The Grimm brothers recorded local fairy tales across Prussia as a form of cultural rebellion against Napoleon and his French army. In fact, their first edition of fairy tales was published in December 1812, right when Napoleon pushed into Russia. This act of cultural pushback was a declaration. These stories represented Germans indirectly proclaiming that they could not be or become French because they were German, with German stories to prove it. After repeated defeats, an exile, and a successful return to power, Napoleon was exiled a second, final time on St. Helena off the west coast of Africa, and he eventually died there, marking an end to an impactful time in global history. In some ways, that ending restored a kind of balance.

But other scales were being tipped outside the political forum. The world of science became weaponized in a way that was not new, but was much more widely transmitted, "like myth, science and reason have an underlying structure: where myth both seeks and supports longevity, science and reason promise access to truth" (Cregan-Reid, 2015, p. 202). Unfortunately, that quest for truth created a new way to wield old power. Science was used to justify racism, genocide, and other crimes against humanity through theories like Social Darwinism. However, science also provided a new lens for humanity to explore self and other. Photography was invented in 1826, developed by French scientist Joseph Nicephore Niepce. This new form of art provided an innovative way to create a window into each other's experiences:

> Both the photograph and the autobiography demonstrate the impossibility of framing our multiple and fragmented selves. They contain levels of authenticity of the subject but not the reality of the subject. Life is an ongoing temporality—the autobiography and the photograph are not. (Cole, 2021, p. 4)

Photography gave humanity a new way to share vulnerability, a new way to create trust and explore.

Creating a new system of governance is no easy feat, particularly when complex regional social, political, and economic practices led to dangerous systems of oppression, including African slavery and Native American genocide. Still, cultural guardians rose up in times of despair with creative ways to overcome. African slaves defied their oppressors through innovative means, including weaving escape routes into their hair and telling stories of hope through Brer Rabbit. "On the plantations, Brer Rabbit, like Anansi in the Caribbean, functioned as a resistance figure for the enslaved whose trickery was aimed at undermining and challenging the plantation regime" (Zobel Marshall, 2019, p. 147); these stories, told in "mixed company," provided a way to transmit hope even when oppressive ears were listening.

In the same vein of hope-based defiance, many Native American tribes refused to bend to the will of Andrew Jackson's Indian Removal. Some tribes tried to remain in their homelands, some hiding in plain sight through marriages to white families, but many were forced to move to Oklahoma. Over time, despair led to a new alliance: a Pan-Nativist movement.

The complexity of the American Civil War cannot be properly captured here; the impact it had on the population of African Americans, Native and Indigenous Americans, women, and Civil War veterans is a hall of mirrors. One certainty is that "the Civil War was a factor in the spread of opiate addiction in America" (Courtwright, 1978, p. 111). John Stith Pemberton, a Confederate States Army veteran and pharmacist, created Coca-Cola to try to cure his opium addiction (Gardiner, 2012) through a nonalcoholic, cocaine-laced drink, although it was ultimately unsuccessful. Pemberton sold his formula and succumbed to his addiction. Coca-Cola continued, with the cocaine being removed from the recipe in 1903 (Liebowitz, 1983). Still, this is notable in that Coca-Cola banked on its unique advertising, its colors linking into the nostalgia of Christmas (Pendergrast, 1993), an association that has maintained and grown throughout time.

This chapter has explored ways in which people used art to express and reinforce their thoughts on revolution. Human responses—grotesque and skewed, but authentic—were also present in the ways in which art was created. Finally, situations were brought forth that might have impacted the way in which art was created, providing a new medium for discussion, a familiar avenue for students to experience historical empathy and grow into their own awareness of our world and their place in it. Table 6.1 provides some ideas to help extend this learning in your classroom.

Table 6.1.

Warmup	Suggested activities	Closing
Lesson 1. Ask students to respond to a prompt by asking, "What items or inventions do you use as part of your daily life in ways that feel as natural as breathing?"	• Students will share the items or inventions they use every day and then begin to brainstorm to answer: 1. What are three ways in which their lives would be different without that item or invention? 2. What are three ways in which the world would be different without that item or invention? • Assessment: Students will discuss if they think any single item or invention could change the course not only of daily life, but also of history, providing evidence to support their argument.	• Quick write. Ask students to create three hashtags to represent their experience in today's lesson.
Lesson 2. Interdependence: Randomly assign students a region from this chapter. Allow time for them to begin to think about partnerships that region had with other regions.	• Allow students to research five to seven examples of their region trading with others. Ask them to identify what is being traded and why the trade is important for people of both regions. • Assessment: Ask students what would happen if something changed in their supply line. What impact would that have on the people of their region and/or diplomacy with other regions?	• To close, ask students to choose ONE emoji that summarizes their thoughts on webs of interdependence of the period. You may also ask them to write a short explanation of their choice.
Lesson 3. Stretching into self-awareness: Ask students, "What 'machines,' figurative or literal, do you feel bound to in your daily life?" Have them share out and discuss.	• Today is about mural-making and contrasts. • Students will need access to art supplies, old magazines, books, and other media, including scratch paper and two-sided tape or glue. • On one side of the medium, students will create a mural to express the machine (figurative or literal) to which they feel bound in their daily lives, and on the other side, they will create a solution to overcoming the machine (figurative or literal). • Students will post, present, or perform their murals.	• Closing: Students will do a quick write comparing their solution to fighting the machine with how other people in this chapter fought against their machine (i.e., Ned Ludd, colonists, French citizens, Toussaint).

References

Baur, J. (1970). International Repercussions of the Haitian Revolution. *The Americas, 26*(4), 394–418.
Bell, A. (2021). The impact of Napoleon Bonaparte in Egypt. *Phi Alpha Theta, 9*. https://digitalcommons.wou.edu/pat/9.
Cole, S. (2021). The autobiography as a photograph. *Academia Letters.* https://doi.org/10.20935/AL187.
Courtwright, D.T. (1978). Opiate addiction as a consequence of the civil war. *Civil War History, 24*(2), 101–111.
Cregan-Reid, V. (2015). *Discovering Gilgamesh: Geology, narrative and the historical sublime in Victorian culture.* Manchester University Press.
Gardiner, R. (2012). The civil war origin of Coca-Cola in Columbus, Georgia. *Muscogiana: Journal of the Muscogee Genealogical Society, 23*, 21–24.
Hoermann, R. (2017). Figures of terror: The "zombie" and the Haitian Revolution. *Atlantic Studies, 14*(2), 152–173.
James, S. (1814). *The History of Toussaint Louverture.* J. Butterworth and Son.
Liebowitz, M.R. (1983). *The chemistry of love.* Little, Brown, & Co.
Merchant, B. (2023). *Blood in the machine: The origins of the rebellion against big tech.* Little Brown and Company.
Mohajan, H. (2019). The first Industrial Revolution: Creation of a new global human era. *Journal of Social Sciences and Humanities, 5*(4), 377–387.
Nhat Hanh, T. (2001). *A pebble for your pocket.* Parallax Press.
Pendergrast, M. (1993). *For God, country and Coca-Cola: The unauthorized history of the great American soft drink and the company that makes it.* Scribner.
Stearns, P.N. (2021). *The industrial revolution in world history* (Fifth edition.). Routledge.
Warren, R. (2017). *Art nouveau and the classical tradition.* Bloomsbury Academic.
Zobel Marshall, E. (2019). *American trickster: Trauma, tradition, and Brer Rabbit.* Rowman & Littlefield.

Chapter Seven

Bullets and Butterfly Wings

*Investigating Imperialism
Circa 1760 CE–1900 CE*

In many ways, this chapter picks up where the previous left off: with Hegel's dialectic remaining suspended without achieving a synthesis. Pushing into "the nineteenth century may be characterised by loss: the loss of lineage, the loss of knowledge, and the loss of narrative," (Cregan-Reid, 2015, p. 210), but with that loss comes a new form of synthesis that completes and continues the earlier dialectic. This chapter tumbles from old imperialism into new, with technological considerations and new interests in the treatment of Indigeneity.

Suggestions for mindfulness aligned to this content are from Jon Kabat-Zinn, a student of Thích Nhất Hạnh (Kabat-Zinn & Hạnh, 2009):

- Ask students to begin finding "I" statements as they explore these lessons that express emotions they are feeling or curiosities they have. Encourage students to think of ways to explore self-inquiry and self-understanding through asking about "I."
- Examples: What do *I* think about these events in history? What do *I* think is right or wrong about what happened? How do *I* feel after reflecting on these events?

GUIDING QUESTIONS

- How did art provide a medium for responses to imperialism?
- How did art reinforce emerging themes of personal and group rights?
- How did art reflect the impact of transoceanic encounters?

The rise of consumerism led to an increase in some workers' wages, which allowed for increased leisure-vacationing; attending performance art and participating in organized sporting activities became parts of life for the wealthy and now, some middle-class, global citizens. Unfortunately, another, darker side of capitalism continued to grow in various forms, one of which was the undeniable, inelastic market of addiction. Addiction: unfavorable for humanity, great for business.

Tea had become a hot commodity for English citizens. Drinking tea as an afternoon snack became part of a ritual that permeated English society and raged at a new, high pitch in the eighteenth century. This led to an unfavorable balance of trade between pricey Chinese tea and English currency. England was desperate for a way to shift profits to their favor, and that happened as English sailors began to trickle opium into the black market from the British Raj of India to China on behalf of the English. This underground market was seen as a distinctly Chinese problem (Bard, 2000) that would only fester with time. At this point, the opium trade was not against the law.

Meanwhile, the Qing Dynasty had other economic and legal trouble brewing in the open sea: Zheng Yi Sao, also known as Madam Ching. Some claim she was the most successful pirate of all time (Sook Duncombe, 2017), and with good reason. While on the sea, Ching ruled the Pirate Confederation that tormented China even as the opium trade continued. Although Madam Ching was represented with the same sorts of fanciful descriptions as other women of power in mythos (see figure 7.1), throughout her career she maintained control of a massive fleet of at least four hundred junks and between forty and sixty thousand pirates (Murray, 2001).

Her knowledge in the execution of policy, diplomacy, and law empowered her. Madam Ching had clear expectations for the rules upon her ships: "anyone caught giving commands on his own or disobeying those of a superior was immediately decapitated" (Murray, 1981, p. 151). These clear and present rules of engagement for her pirates served Madam Ching well and contributed to her success on and off the seas. With a sophisticated understanding of diplomacy, Madam Ching made tremendous amounts of capital and negotiated surrender on her own terms—leaving piracy for a private life of retirement in ways she, and not the government, dictated (Sook Duncombe, 2017).

An understanding of the importance of legalities was also a point of concern for King Kamehameha III, who "created the Kingdom of Hawaii's first series of written laws" (Merry, 2000, p. 78). This, along with his declaration of human rights, might have been an offensive effort to formalize Hawaiian tradition in a way that bowed to Western practice and tried to preserve culture for his already-dwindling population. Kamehameha III was known for his cleverness—he used diplomacy and international relations to restore

Figure 7.1. Zheng Yi Sao

Hawaiian independence after it was lost to the British, one of many attempted takeovers by other, more powerful nations (Riconda, 1972). Kamehameha III continued his reign, maintaining power in his nation through adhering to new, Western traditions (see figure 7.2) while preserving the traditions of Hawaii in ways that could be seen as weaving together their past and the global future that awaited.

Four short years after Kamehameha's death, a law was passed by the Hawaiian Evangelical Association banning the hula (Silva, 2000); this sparked a series of restrictive events for Native Hawaiians, a beginning of the end of their traditional way of life.

The Qing Dynasty, in its desperation to eradicate opium use, appointed Lin Zexu as viceroy. Zexu's letter to Queen Victoria pled with her to think of her role as a Christian monarch and that she would not want to subject her own people to such a horrid fate as what awaited opium eaters (Teng & Fairbank, 1979). Even as Zexu's pleas fell on deaf ears, other parts of the world were listening.

Figure 7.2. The Kamehameha Royal Family, c. 1835.

As the opium trade wars were on the horizon, Japan had long since closed its doors to the outside world, with small exceptions made for the Dutch. In 1635, the Sakoku Edict forbade leaving or entering Japan, as well as the practice of Christianity. This restrictive environment lent itself to a unique form of isolation that in many ways allowed Japan to return to and remain in the medieval period. It was in that setting that Katsushika Hokusai was able to create the Great Wave off Kanagawa (see figure 7.3), perhaps the most reproduced piece of art throughout time (Wood, 2017); in many ways it remains an artistic fossil of what life was like in isolated Japan.

Hokusai could not have known that twenty-one short years later, Matthew Perry would forcibly open Japan to the West (Fillmore, 1852) and one year later sign a forced treaty with the United States at the Convention of Kanagawa. Such an event takes the meaning of the Great Wave and turns the idea around into a new, certainly unintended meaning.

Still, the British continued the opium trade, fighting wars with China over its distribution and sale. After the First and Second Opium Wars and an ultimate British victory, the Treaty of Nanking ceded Hong Kong to the British. Then the Treaty of Tienstin required China to pay war reparations, among other concessions, such as extraterritoriality for Westerners. This ongoing "century of shame" for China raised a continued cry that would resonate into the twentieth century, and maybe even beyond.

Figure 7.3. The Great Wave off Kanagawa by Katsushika Hokusai, c. 1831.

The impacts of the opium trade on the global market were not restricted to relations between China and Great Britain; India also challenged colonial oppressors with the First War of Independence, also called the Sepoy Mutiny. With the loss of autonomy and the banning of cultural practices tightening on all levels, Lakshmibai, the Rani of Jhansi, along with others of the nobility, fought the British for control of India. Ultimately the rebellion failed, leading to a loss for India, but also the loss of the Rani, who was badly wounded in battle. Before her death, a British reporter described her as "personable, clever and beautiful," as well as "the most dangerous of all Indian leaders" (David, 2003, p. 367), a reverence that is evident in the arts that depict her (see figure 7.4). Her story and image became legendary, cementing her in history as a patriotic and fearless freedom fighter (Sen, 2007, p. 1761) for Indian independence.

Like Rani and the people of India, citizens of Crimea found themselves at an intersectional point of dissolving and increasing powerhouses. The site of the ancient Greek city of Chersonesus became the grounds for the foundation of the "Eastern Question" of the stability and sustainability of the Ottoman Empire. Battles of the Crimean War also marked the dangerous transitional point that turned warfare more toward modern methodologies of communications in and around battle, including the use of the telegraph, railways, and photographs. However, the Crimean War also led to a new development in

Figure 7.4. Portrait of Lakshmibai, the Rani of Jhansi, by Ratan Kushwah. 1861.

care: the professionalization of nursing was initiated there by Florence Nightingale, who later began the first formal, secular school for nursing (Petroni, 1969). The Crimean War in many ways marked the start of good and bad storylines that would also continue into the next century.

Likewise, farther south, the scramble for Africa shifted the continent into a new form of concern—resource mining. When African slavery was banned by Great Britain, the United States, and other European nations, thoughts from industrious minds turned from a coercive labor grab toward the stripping of natural resources. African tribes responded to imperialism by turning to tradition, uniting, applying diplomatic maneuvers, and finally going to battle. These responses are all embodied in the Battle of Adwa. First, tribal leaders attempted to appeal to religious practices they had in common with Italians, reminding them that Ethiopia had been practicing Christianity for centuries. Then Ethiopian tribal leaders united and finally went to war (figure 7.5). As you can see in this painting, the artist is expressing that the Ethiopians had both guns and God on their side in this battle. Tribes in Ethiopia remained free of imperialistic presence (Woldeyes, 2020), while elsewhere, tribes suffered a much different fate.

Children were also subject to the ideals of imperialism through published storybooks. *The Jungle Book* and other stories reinforced imperialism as a desired state of being for those ruled by the British. This was a common practice that was either intentional or accidental during the time (Kutzer, 2000). Still others used fiction as a way to speak out against slavery and against imperialism. *The Lowest Animal*, by Mark Twain, described the animals in a zoo as having more humanity than the men in the zoo, an expression of his disgust of the time in which he lived (Kaplan, 1991).

Figure 7.5. Battle of Adwa the scenery of the battle on a mountains view, author unknown, c. 1889.

Genocide also marked the period. The Ottoman Empire was facing not only a dissolution of power through outside pressures, but also internal ones. The Young Turks both challenged the Ottoman Empire and sparked the Armenian genocide (Lewy, 2005). This instability caused migrations to the Americas and a legacy that continues to impact pop culture, including calls for awareness and continued, present advocacy by musicians like System of a Down.

In the Americas, Native Americans were being forcibly removed from their homelands and killed in a series of actions that some would call genocide while others maintain the definition does not fit. The truth remains that Native peoples were not only oppressed by political events, including the Indian Removal Act, but their stories, and in some cases the identities of their descendants, were collectively silenced. The largest mass execution of Indigenous people in American history was ordered by Abraham Lincoln in 1862, a month before he signed the Emancipation Proclamation. With little resources, limited space, and only tradition to turn to, some tribes united in solidarity to dance. The Ghost Dance became an essential moment not only in the Pan-Nativist movement, but also in a religious revolt used to inspire and revitalize what remained of an identified Native population (Martin, 1991).

The Kingdom of Hawaii experienced continued static as more powerful nations persisted in pressing into their lands. Many Native Hawaiians refused to work on the Dole Plantations in a show of cultural solidarity, which led to a growth in the number of Korean, Japanese, and Vietnamese immigrants working on those plantations instead. That in turn led to the formation of ethnically based gangs intended to protect and defend those with common nations of origin who were working the fields. The surge in fruit production fertilized the urge for annexation, cultivated by Sanford Dole. Queen Liliuokalani protested annexation by attempting diplomacy, reaching out to the United States government to no avail. She was ultimately imprisoned. During these transitional times, she wrote, "Aloha'Oe," a sorrowful ballad that served as a final goodbye to traditional Hawaiian culture.

This chapter explored ways in which art provided a medium for responses to imperialism. Songs and visual arts gave a place for expression when diplomacy and the letter of the law failed. Through art, people of the time were able to express what they were feeling; art provided a medium for agency. Finally, art here represented a way to capture the feelings and events of transoceanic encounters. Table 7.1 presents some suggested activities for you; the invitation is there to make these yours as you bring this content into your classroom.

Table 7.1

Warmup	Suggested activities	Closing
Lesson 1. Ask students, "What are some traditions in your life that bring you comfort or connection?"	• Ask students to create a list of collected traditions from their classmates and find themes among them. Then ask students to research the traditions the peoples in this chapter practiced. • Assessment: Ask students to create a Venn diagram comparing the traditions between two groups from the chapter. Then ask students to compare what was similar between the two and compare that to their own tradition. What was the same? What was different?	• Exit ticket: Students will do a quick write on how they would feel if their tradition was suddenly against the law. How would they respond? Why?
Lesson 2. Ask students, "What kinds of responses do people have to new ideas that feel restrictive?"	• Ask students to discuss these responses and then compare those to the responses of people in the chapter. • Then ask students to choose one group of people who responded to imperialism in the chapter; would their history have been different if they had responded to imperialism in a different way? How? Find three impacts and hypothesize different outcomes.	• Journaling: The students will write a journal reflecting on the impact of responses to imperialism.
Lesson 3. Ask students, "Which form of art do you think has the most impact to express rebellion or support in today's world? Why?" Allow students to share out and discuss.	• Create files with banks of information that include art that was explored in this chapter. Then, using flexible grouping, ask students to become subject-matter experts not only on that piece of art, but also determining whether they think that medium of art was impactful to the people of the time. They should have three reasons to support their answer.	• Human scale. Ask students to present their discussion to the class, citing ways in which a certain artistic medium is impactful to others in showing support or rebellion. Have students arrange themselves according to the discussion they agree with—their opinions may be changed as the discussion continues so they may continue to move throughout the activity as new ideas are brought forth.

References

Bard, S. (2000). Tea and opium. *Journal of Hong Kong Branch of the Royal Asiatic Society, 40*, 1–19.

Cregan-Reid, V. (2015). *Discovering Gilgamesh: Geology, narrative and the historical sublime in Victorian culture*. Manchester University Press.

David, S. (2003). *The Indian Mutiny: 1857*. Penguin.

Fillmore, M. (November 13, 1852). *Letters from U.S. President Millard Fillmore and U.S. Navy Commodore Matthew C. Perry to the Emperor of Japan (1852–1853)*. Columbia University.

Kabat-Zinn, J., and Hanh, T.N. (2009). *Full catastrophe living: Using the wisdom of your body and mind to face stress, pain, and illness*. Random House.

Kaplan, J. (1991). *Mr. Clemens and Mark Twain: A biography*. Simon & Schuster.

Kutzer, M.D. (2000). *Empire's children: Empire and imperialism in classic British children's books*. Routledge.

Lewy, G. (2005). Revisiting the Armenian genocide. *Insight Turkey, 7*(3), 89–99.

Martin, J.W. (1991). Before and beyond the Sioux Ghost Dance: Native American prophetic movements and the study of religion. *Journal of the American Academy of Religion, 59*(4), 677–701.

Merry, S.E. (2000). *Colonizing Hawai'i: The cultural power of law*. Princeton University Press.

Murray, D. (1981). One woman's rise to power: Cheng I's wife and the pirates. *Historical Reflections, 8*(3), 147–161.

Petroni, A. (1969). The first nursing school in the world—St. Thomas Hospital School in London. *Munca Sanit, 17*(8), 449–454.

Riconda, D. (April 25, 1972). *Thomas Square nomination form*. National Register of Historic Places. U.S. National Park Service.

Sen, I. (2007). Inscribing the Rani of Jhansi in colonial 'mutiny' fiction. *Economic and Political Weekly, 42*(19), 1754–1761.

Silva, N.K. (2000). Kanawai e ho'opau I na hula kuolo Hawai'i: The political economy of banning the hula. *Hawaiian Journal of History, 38*, 29–48.

Sook Duncombe, L. (2019). *Pirate women: The princesses, prostitutes, and privateers who ruled the seven seas*. Chicago Review Press.

Teng, S., & Fairbank, J.K. (1979). *China's response to the West: A documentary survey, 1839–1923*. Harvard University Press.

Woldeyes, Y.G. (29 February 2020). The battle of Adwa: An Ethiopian victory that ran against the current of colonialism. *Conversation*.

Wood, P. (20 July 2017). Is this the most reproduced artwork in history? ABC News.

Chapter Eight

Standing Alone
Pre- and Post-World War I

The close of the nineteenth century created an event horizon on many fronts: one being the mythicization of the previous period, and the other the genesis of a new age of necropolitics, "new and unique forms of social existence in which vast populations are subjected to living conditions that confer upon them the status of the living dead" (Mbembé, 2003, p. 40). As Indigenous communities and others continuing to be impacted by imperialism saw the twilight of their traditional ways of life, others found fear in different ways, stirring the beginnings of what would eventually become World War I.

Suggestions for mindfulness aligned to this content are adapted from Chödrön (2006):

QUESTIONS

- When is there an urge to bear down (or get hooked, also called *shenpa*) on the negative feelings evoked by topics?
- How can identifying the places and topics that activate *shenpa* (or hooking) help refocus thought patterns from aggression toward activating historical empathy?
- How can stopping to pause and breathe lead to different solutions and feelings rather than typical, habitual responses to things like war and aggression?

GUIDING QUESTIONS

- How did art provide a medium for expressing understanding for the changing times of pre–World War I?
- How did art provide evidence of individual experiences during and after World War I?

Although draped in the legacy of an altered past, the American West held uncomfortable realities and questions for new settlers. For example, the question of whether or not Indigenous people, here called "Indians," were really people at all was settled for some in a court case, *Standing Bear v. Cook*. The judge in this landmark civil-rights case determined that "an Indian is a person within the meaning of the laws of the United States" and could not be forcibly moved or confined to a reservation (Dando-Collins, 2004). This was a striking juxtaposition from earlier diplomatic moves from the United States government. While some saw the end of an era in the taming of the Wild West, others saw opportunity. Turning attentions to the American West provided "a place for the pressure valve of North/South relations to be eased in a collective, redemptive move toward 'civilizing the west' that allowed for unity between those who had fought against each other in the civil war" (Stallones Marshall, 2022). Buffalo Bill's Wild West show provided work for over one thousand performers, some of whom included Sitting Bull (see figure 8.1), Red Cloud, and Chief Joseph.

These shows were largely exploitive (McNenly, 2012), but the chance to perform was sometimes welcome to tribespeople who were looking for new opportunities. The legacy of these reenactments in some ways continues to the present, through faulty textbook narratives and stories, a testament to the impact of performance art on collective memory.

The transportation revolution persisted with the first successful flights by the Wright brothers in Kitty Hawk, North Carolina, providing an entirely new stream of consideration for travel and exploration. Although transportation was previously thought to provide a new foundation for social equality, stratification systems quickly became reinforced as evident in *The Steerage*, seen in figure 8.2.

Much has been studied about this photograph, including the citizenship of pictured subjects who were at one time thought to be a collection of those turned away from the United States for failure to pass health or employment requirements; however, it is more likely that they were traveling to Europe from America on temporary working visas that may have been related to a construction boom of the time (Whelan, 2000). It is notable when inspecting this photograph to see there is a sense of bustle, but also a kind of gendered

Figure 8.1. Sitting Bull and Buffalo Bill by William Notman Studios, 1895.

Figure 8.2. The Steerage, photograph by Alfred Stieglitz in 1907.

line as well. The men at the top seem to outnumber the women, and the women below are in different kinds of dress than those on the top. However, women are the dominate gender belowdecks, a stark reminder that gender stratification has, perhaps always, existed on a continuum (Lesser Blumberg, 1984).

Explorations and exploitations of places unknown continued, as well as competition for firsts and ownership. Disputed missions to the North Pole began and with those, an exploration of cultures surrounding there. The grapple for hegemony reached into construction work with the assembling of the *Titanic*, which lasted over three years. Then competition for maritime excellence slammed to a gruesome halt with the sinking of the *Titanic* in 1912 after it hit an iceberg.

Political collisions continued in Mexico as a rash of revolutionary battles raged across the country. Women took up arms as women, *soldaderas* (see figure 8.3), "in many respects, the Mexican revolution was not only a men's but a women's revolution" (Katz, 1998, p. 290).

At times, the women would hide their identities—trying to identify as male by appearing more masculine and claiming to be men; in those instances, some of their commanders knew their true identities. Ángela Jiménez, for example, used her gender to her advantage (Salas, 1990), using her womanhood to get out of jail, working in disguise as a spy; she also served as a spokesperson for the *soldaderas*, and even with her gender being known, she was promoted to lieutenant in her division. Ángela's story, like so many others, helped reinforce notions of gender equality, which led Mexican president Venustiano Carranza to create reforms on the legal status of women (Mirande & Evangelina, 1981).

Tangible tension had been rising globally for decades, with the arms race reaching a fever pitch in the early twentieth century. Weapons started being developed at an accelerated pace, leading to a rise in militarism and industry. New forms of terrorism, espionage, and battle strategies among other

Figure 8.3. Soldaderas, unknown photographer, date unknown.

maneuvers made the Napoleonic Wars seem like a far-away time rather than a mere hundred years earlier.

There was, of course, nationalism and imperialism to blame for rising static among nations, but there was also a lesser-named social component at play: fear. It is well-known that Germany had been fearful of being taken over for a long time. Public speeches such as the Hammer and Anvil Speech of 1899, as well as other private expressions of fear, proved to be hallmarks of German leadership. It was said that Kaiser Wilhelm told his gardener not to bother planting trees in one area of his home since the Russians would be there invading soon anyway; then, when Wilhelm declared war, those in attendance noticed tears in his eyes (Berghahn, 1994). When one pauses to consider the role of fear in war, something shifts in the perception of things to come.

It is also notable that this "Great War" started with what many people would call an act of terrorism (Green, 2012), committed by someone who was around the same age as a modern-day recent high school graduate. Gavrilo Princip was nineteen years old when he killed the Archduke of Austria-Hungary, his wife, and their unborn child, sparking a series of events that started World War I. Discussing gravitas moments like that make it easy to become "hooked" and turn in to the aggression, but this provides a wonderful moment to stop and think with students. Consider posing these questions:

- Do you think Gavrilo understood the impact his actions would have?
- Do you think he was afraid of something or someone in his own community and that that fear led him to join the Black Hand?
- Consider his responses and reactions after he was caught: he cried as he apologized for killing the Archduke's wife and child. Was he a child making grown-up decisions or an adult making grown-up decisions? Why?
- Is there ever a point when you are no longer responsible for your decisions?
- What about intention—does that count for anything?
- What if you make a big mistake when you are young—what happens then?
- Can you ever atone for your mistakes? How?

These are the kinds of questions that will really get your students thinking and talking and thinking and talking some more. This can also, perhaps more importantly, get students to start thinking about what wars are like on a micro, rather than a macro level.

Another unexpected social impact of war included the ways that war changed fashion, particularly for women. Corsets had been a part of women's wear for centuries, but shortly after the start of World War I, women began to be encouraged not to buy or wear them to free up materials for weapons. This and other shifts in the roles of women led to the death of widespread corset usage and the rise of the brassiere (Farrell-Beck & Gau, 2002).

Three years after the sinking of the *Titanic*, another maritime tragedy struck when a German U-boat sank a rival company's passenger ship, the *Lusitania*. The loss of life in both tragedies is still being investigated to better understand human responses to emergency situations (Frey et al., 2010). The raw, human responses to loss were activated in the United States public arena with the publishing of Fred Spear's artwork, *Enlist*, one month after the sinking of the *Lusitania* (see figure 8.4).

Figure 8.4. Enlist, art by Fred Spear, 1915.

As you can see, there is no mention of who or what has caused the circumstance in which the woman and her baby find themselves as they slowly come to the end of their lives, together, but the knowledge that something like this could have happened on the *Lusitania* had the intended effect, contributing to a sense of desperation in the American public to join the now-raging World War I, to seek vengeance for those lost lives.

Stories of humanity shining through despite warfare abound throughout the tragic timeline of World War I. The Christmas Truce in 1914 was a wonderfully recounted pause in a war of attrition, leading to an unexpected soccer game between the British and the Germans, with the Germans winning the game 2–1 (Woodcock, 2013). Soldiers from both sides of the trench reported on the joy they felt in those moments in the letters they wrote back home. The experiences of war, like most things, can lead to different responses in different people. For example, several notable artists served as ambulance drivers; Ernest Hemingway, Walt Disney, and Olive Mudie-Cooke, among countless others, took away different events and memories that later impacted the course of their lives. Mudie-Cooke captured her experiences in watercolors and other works, like that in figure 8.5.

In the painting, Mudie-Cooke expresses a kind of moment through the colors she chose to highlight the lighting of the cigarette. The focal point then becomes a kind of warm hearth the volunteer is creating for the wounded soldier, but there is also a sense of evanescence to the moment, expressed through the flowing brushstrokes of the image. Other artists were serving on the Central Front, including Adolf Hitler.

Conflict on a global scale was also complicating matters for those in Russia, where internal strife was reaching a fever pitch. With cyclical famine and what felt like incompetent leadership in the Romanovs, taken in tandem with increasing pressure from outside, the Bolsheviks rose in the February revolution, the abdication of the tsar, and later October revolutions, promising "peace, land, and bread" in a cry that for many felt like a solution to generations-old issues that had plagued their people. And even though the Romanovs had abdicated, and even though they were related to the powerful royal family in Great Britain, their family and the legacy of the Romanovs died together in July 1918.

The Spanish flu outbreak rose as the Romanovs fell, blanketing the world in another kind of hopelessness. Letters, diary entries, and newspaper articles described a population that felt as though God were punishing the world, and in fear people turned to coping mechanisms like ignoring the pandemic or isolation to save those they loved. Artists grappled to convey that experience even as the war raged on. Expressionist and queer artist (Izenberg, 2006) Egon Schiele was one of thousands who succumbed to the Spanish

Figure 8.5. A World War One Voluntary Aid Detachment nurse lighting a cigarette for a patient inside an ambulance, watercolor by Olive Mudie-Cooke, date unknown.

flu, although his art continued to be displayed in galleries across Europe, a testament to the lasting marks made by the art world. The pandemic in many ways froze singular moments that would in time become relevant again in unexpected ways.

After years of human cost and consequence, on November 11, 1918, World War I ended. Soon after, in 1920, the Nineteenth Amendment passed in the United States, creating a new path for American women to use voice and choice in their lives. Still, sexual segregation continued. For example, in Australia post–World War I, cultural practices excluded women from working or drinking in pubs (Kirby, 2003). In 1922, the first documentary film was released, *Nanook of the North*, which brought forth new questions of what it meant to document something as an observer, how difficult it could be to not interfere with something one is documenting, and whether one should interact or interfere at all. Standing alone continued as Charles Lindbergh completed the first nonstop flight from New York City to Paris in 1927. That same year, Knud Rasmussen trekked across North America with a dogsled team, starting an exploration of Inuit cultures that he documented in several volumes of research.

New explorations of what humanity could be capable of, for good, continued a snowball effect of discovery. In medicine, insulin began to be used as a treatment in 1921. That, along with the discovery of penicillin, began to change the shape of modern medicine, providing hope in the aftermath of so much death and war.

Standing alone provided a framework for this chapter's exploration of World War I. Mindfulness suggestions challenged the idea that instead of leaning into feelings of aggression, war could be reexamined in a more thoughtful way, including mindfully examining the impact of war on the individual. The chapter explored ways that art provided a medium for understanding, activating, and expressing unique experiences in a time of collective strife. There are ideas in table 8.1 for how to bring this content into your classroom. Remember that these are not prescriptive or exhaustive lesson plans; please modify according to your and your students' needs.

Table 8.1.

Warmup	Suggested activities	Closing
Lesson 1. Ask students, "What can we learn from a timeline?" Have them share out and discuss.	• Brainstorm events before, during, and after World War I. Where are causes and consequences represented in those events? Students will construct a timeline based on the events provided in the brainstorm. • Extend their learning: Ask students, "How can a timeline help illustrate the linear and nonlinear nature of decision-making in times of war?"	• Exit ticket: Students will identify a pivotal moment in their own lives and create a timeline around it. Now compare that to an event in World War I.
Lesson 2. Ask students, "Does art provide information on feelings? How do you know?" Allow time for consideration and discussion.	• Choose one piece of art from this unit to use as an example of finding emotion in art; then allow students to find a unique piece of art to use for today's activity and allow them to explore it independently. • Assessment: Ask students to identify the feeling they see expressed in the art and explain their reasoning; then have them tie these feelings from the artist to the social, political, and/or economic circumstances in which the art was created.	• Turn and talk. Ask students whether they think it is important to identify emotions, then ask, "Why? Why not?" Ask students to share out or do a "parking lot" post it to close.
Lesson 3. Ask students, "Do you think art influences displays of power in today's world? Why? How?" Allow students to share out and discuss.	• Create files with banks of information that include maps, rulers, timelines, and ideologies of the different players in this chapter. Then, using flexible grouping, ask students to become subject-matter experts not only on the art of the region or people, but also thinking about how political power from surrounding areas might have influenced that artist. • Assessment: students create a visual representation (an "artifact") of the power of the region in which the artist(s) they researched lived and created, then ask them to share out, looking for similarities.	• Quick write. Ask students to create a thesis statement on the impact political power has on the art that is created in a region.

References

Berghahn, V.R. (1994). *Imperial Germany, 1871–1914: Economy, society, culture, and politics.* Berghahn Books.

Chödrön, P. (2006). *Practicing peace in times of war: A Buddhist perspective.* Shambhala.

Dando-Collins, S. (2004). The newspaper edito. In *Standing Bear is a person: The true story of a Native American's quest for justice*, pp. 51–60. Cambridge.

Farrell-Beck, J., & Gau, C. (2002). *Uplift: The bra in America.* University of Pennsylvania.

Frey, B.S., Savagec, D.A., & Torglerb, B. (2010). Interaction of natural survival instincts and internalized social norms exploring the *Titanic* and *Lusitania* disasters. *Proceedings of the National Academy of Sciences, 107*(11), 4862–4865.

Green, J. (2012, September 27). *Archdukes, cynicism, and World War I.* Crash Course. https://www.youtube.com/watch?v=_XPZQ0LAlR4.

Izenberg, G.N. (2006). Egon Schiele: Expressionist art and masculine crisis. *Psychoanalytic Inquiry, 26*(3), 462–483.

Katz, F. (1998). *The life and times of Pancho Villa.* Stanford University Press.

Kirby, D. (2003). "Beer, glorious beer": Gender politics and Australian popular culture. *Journal of Popular Culture, 37*(2), 244–256.

Lesser Blumberg, R. (1984). A general theory of gender stratification. *Sociological Theory, 2*, 23–101.

Mbembé, J.A. (translation by: Meintjes, L.). (2003). Necropolitics. *Public Culture, 15*(1), 11–40.

McNenly, L.S. (2012). *Native performers in wild west shows: From Buffalo Bill to Euro Disney.* University of Oklahoma Press.

Mirande, A., & Evangelina, E. (1981). *La Chicana: The Mexican American woman.* Chicago Press.

Salas, E. (1990). *Soldaderas in the Mexican Revolution.* University of Texas Press.

Stallones Marshall, L. (2022, July 30). *Fighting the frontier: Disrupting Indigenous erasure in the history classroom.* [Lecture notes]. Keynote speech. Florida Council for History Education.

Whelan, R. (2000). *Stieglitz on photography: His selected essays and notes.* Aperture.

Woodcock, J. (17 November 2013). England v Germany: When rivals staged beautiful game on the Somme. *Daily Telegraph.*

Chapter Nine

The Space Between Our Wicked Lies
The Great Depression and World War II, 1930–1945

The problem with the time leading up to and within World War II is the problem with most lies: they find their ways into holes and hurts in structures that were previously seen as solid truths. After all, "there are years that ask questions and years that answer" (Hurston, 1937, p. 21). That sentiment rings true here, along with unspoken questions and the duality of silence. With fascism rising in Germany, Italy, and Russia, and a general distrust of each other, along with a reaffirming of isolationism in the aftermath of World War I, the Great Depression took its toll on social, political, and economic energy streams in personal and global ways. Blame, humiliation, and hunger grew in places where citizens were punished for the decisions of their leaders. In desperation, people turned toward fascist and populist leadership (Kaltwasser et al., 2020) they may have rejected under different circumstances; the rest, as they say, is history.

Suggestions for mindfulness aligned to this content are adapted from a tonglen meditation provided by Chödrön (2009).

QUESTIONS

- How can you use the breath to allow yourself to acknowledge and sit in the discomfort of an unfortunate situation?
- How can you use the breath to create an exchange from a perception of discomfort to a reaffirmation of power and hope?
- A suggestion from Chödrön (2009) states:

    in the in-breath you breathe in with the wish to take away the suffering, and breathe out with the wish to send comfort and happiness to the same people, animals, nations, or whatever it is you decide. Do this for an individual, or do this for large areas, and if you do this with more than one subject in mind, that's fine ... breathing in as fully as you can, radiating out as widely as you can.

- Making this work: Consider taking the content of the chapter in pieces. This may allow spaces for moments of mindfulness with the breath to process what is happening and create a more enriching understanding of the content and of the self-noticing ways the breath supports a response of exchange, leading to a further understanding of self and allowing for a more empathetic view of the content of the chapter.

GUIDING QUESTIONS

- How did art express the human costs of the Great Depression?
- How did art reinforce emerging themes of social, political, and economic impacts of World War II?
- How did art reflect the changes in science as an effect of World War II?

There is often a misconception that the Great Depression was caused by the stock market crash of 1929. Although that was a contributing factor, it was not the sole, or even the most pressing, cause. Instead, consider first the Quiet Depression of overtaxed and overly indebted farmers (Green, 2013). World War I had created a demand for increased crops, which led many farmers to turn from their reliance on "farm power that was mainly furnished by horses and mules" (Barton & Cooper, 1948, p. 117) toward tractors—and borrowing money to purchase them—that then led to immediate increases in crop yields. But over time in, overused soil, and even drought caused an agricultural crisis that impacted everyone. In various parts of the world including Germany, there was a "deficiency in agricultural production" (Bresciani-Turroni, 2003, p. 195) after World War I that led to snowballing issues of inflation, thereby causing social and economic hardship. Still, "in spite of their reckless borrowing spree, especially during the postwar boom, farmers were more a victim of the depression than a cause of it" (Ferderico, 2005, p. 976). Farmers and citizens alike suffered the consequences of the Great Depression. Here, hunger shifts from being a regional concern to an indicator of global social, political, and economic imbalances (Jachertz & Nützenadel, 2011).

Nevertheless, in places like the United States, artists were still working, largely due to their salaries being provided as part of the Works Progress Administration in the New Deal. Dorothea Lange is credited with using her photography to help humanize the Great Depression (Trigg, 2023) in works such as *Migrant Mother* (see figure 9.1).

Figure 9.1. Migrant mother, photographed by Dorothea Lange, 1936.

Despite the problematic undertones that surround this photograph of an Indigenous woman and her children, including issues of realism and witnessing (Langford, 2016), there is power in Lange's capture of this experience. This and other photographs like it offer a plethora of information about the varied and strenuous situations of people living through the Depression. This is particularly telling since the experience of Native and Indigenous

Americans was largely being ignored by cultural anthropologists and historians of the time (Edmunds, 1995). *Migrant Mother* is an essential snapshot, not only for the raw emotion of the mother who was pictured, Florence Thompson, but also for the imagery Lange was trying to express in her work. In this and the series of shots taken before this photograph, Lange attempted to capture the feelings of strife, desperation, and uncertainty that so many women and mothers were experiencing during the Depression.

Women and mothers framed the archetype of the women that Italy's Benito Mussolini and Russia's Joseph Stalin had in mind to support their regimes. Stalin used women like "the world's first woman ambassador," Aleksandra Kollontai (Farnsworth, 2010), as ways to publicize and propagate his support of women in power. This twisted, anti-feminist/feminist ideology fed into the cultural fabric of many fascist regimes, and

> Mussolini was the innovator or inventor of the relation between women and fascism; his early speeches, dating from 1922–1923, were directed to obtaining the support of women, which was a fundamental element in the consent needed for the "seizure of power." (Macciocchi, 1979, p. 69)

Picasso saw this theme firsthand and reclaimed it in his art as an act of rebellion and defiance. Women, in general, and mothers and children were used as the focal point of one of the most striking pieces of anti-war art in history (Preston, 2012), *Guernica* by Pablo Picasso. The painting features the horrors of the aftermath of the bombing of the village of Guernica by Nazi Germany and Fascist Italy at the request of Spanish Nationalists. Picasso created this work to raise funds and awareness of the Spanish Civil War (Cole, 2021) and to show his disdain for the rise of Spanish fascist Francisco Franco. Picasso created *Guernica* as a means of rebellion, using symbolism in his sometimes-obtuse, sometimes-obvious art to express "the threat posed to Western civilisation by war" (Keen, 1980, p. 469).

Ironically, Hitler was also an artist. The same Western civilization that Picasso and other artists clung to as their framework to rebellion against fascism and other forms of oppression was the same Western civilization that Hitler used as a justification for his push for cultural hegemony in Germany (Goeschel, 2018, p. 65). Hitler and others saw adolescent crime gangs and young female prostitutes flooding the streets of Germany during the Great Depression (Gellately & Stolzfus, 2001). However, as Hitler's Nazi Party grew, so did his encouragement of "violent masculinity" (Cushman, 2021), but Hitler "affirmed that in politics, it is necessary to have the support of women, because the men will follow spontaneously" (Macciocchi, 1979, p. 69). Hitler also banked on adolescent vulnerability as an untapped resource, using youth who had not yet learned to think for themselves (Harrer, 2007) as well as a confusing, progressive series of farming initiatives (Snyder, 2010) to spark the collective interest of the globe. This curiosity about German happenings focused on positive areas of interest, citizens saw what Hitler wanted them to see, even as his ideological shift rapidly increased in a movement toward genocide (Gellately & Stolzfus, 2001).

The passing of the Enabling Act (Stackelberg & Winkle, 2002) accelerated the phases of genocide as Hitler began isolating Jewish people from society. Here again, he found cracks in a recently ailing society, amplifying previously existing discriminatory practices (Fein, 1979) to gain traction and leveraging that rhetoric to give himself and his party more power.

Even then, the stirrings of Resistance were felt throughout the Jewish community as the Youth Aliyah was established and quickly "rescued about five thousand Children and Youth . . . from the Nazis before the outbreak of World War Two" (Hacohen, 2001, p. 216). Still, World War Two and the Shoah (Gilad, 2019), the Holocaust, began. Nazis systematically isolated, moved, and murdered one-third of the global Jewish population, ethnic Poles, Slavs, Romani people, homosexuals, Afro-Germans, and others.

Memoirs abound from those in and around the Holocaust, creative artifacts standing as a testament to the experiences of those writers who were unwillingly caught in the chaos. Each work provides a mirror, window, or sliding-glass door (Sims-Bishop, 1990)—like the remarkable *Diary of a Young Girl* by Anne Frank (Frank & O'Brien, 2020), or the lesser-known *Memoirs from the Warsaw Ghetto* by Vladka Meed (1979). Each work provides an authentic perspective of life during the Holocaust. Meed provides a recounting of her life as a young Jewish woman and her family, who initially trusted the Germans but were later all killed in concentration camps. Vladka escaped by chance and later joined the Resistance movement. Her story is not isolated because "the Nazi image of a Jew was a man . . . they did not perceive women as being carriers in the Resistance which made it easier for women to help others around them" (Cushman, 2021), and her story also provides complexity, exploring difficult family dynamics that were amplified by the impossible circumstances of the Holocaust.

A similarly intricate story that navigates the family dynamics of Holocaust victims and survivors is expressed in *The Complete Maus: A Survivor's Tale* (Spiegel, 1996). The writer, Art Spiegel, lost his brother due to a tragedy related to the threat of a roundup and transport of his family members, a trauma his parents long denied ever happened. Spiegel described having a kind of sibling rivalry with his "ghost brother" (Hirsch, 2011, p. 37), who had been lost in the Holocaust, and the impact that continued mourning had on his relationship with his parents. Spiegel used Maus as a way to capture his family's experience and to try to find a deeper connection with his parents, especially his father.

For those who were imprisoned, art had a "fonction de sauvetage," a "life-saving function" (Richard, 1995, p. 216). By creating art, one could maintain a sense of self and preservation of story in case of almost-certain calamity (Bohm-Duchen, 2014). Consider the piece in figure 9.2, drawn by Amalie Seckbach. This, and her other works, can be found in the Ghetto Fighters House Archives. These visual art pieces remind us of Amalie's legacy as an artist, her visual creations, her life, and her lived experiences before and during the Holocaust.

Figure 9.2. Young Woman with a Crown Among Flowers, Color pencil and pastel on paper, drawn by Amalie Seckbach during imprisonment in Theresienstadt. November 15, 1943.

Despite rumblings in the Pacific, the United States remained firmly in their isolationist stance until the surprise attack of Pearl Harbor (Morison, 2001). Here, long moments of disaster provide space for a blurred form of art, film footage, which can be found on YouTube. Published by Naval History and Heritage, "Pearl Harbor Attack Footage (1941)" provides a silent, black-and-white reel of the events of that day, an attempt to preserve and sustain the memory of what happened for whatever, and whomever, was to come later.

After the bombing of Pearl Harbor, Japanese American citizens in Hawaii and the continental United States (Okihiro, 2005) faced suspicion from their own country, leading to an unjust mass incarceration (Nagata et al., 2019). Here, Japanese American internees used art to "create a livable space for survival," "make connections," and "enhance their chances of mental survival" (Dusselier, 2005, pp. 159–60). Artists like George Matsusaburo Hibi, Charles Isamu Morimoto, among countless others, including the creator of figure 9.3, used art to preserve and continue. Later memoirs again have provided insight into the imprint these experiences left on young Japanese American children, including *A Farewell to Manzanar* (Houston & Houston, 2017) and *They Called Us Enemy* (Takei et al., 2019). Art provided a medium of agency, hope, and even rebellion—creating art was, indeed, a way to survive.

Artistic imagery can sometimes act as a lifesaver in unexpected ways. Throughout World War II, pinup-girl art abounded, with their wallet-sized images tucked into pockets, even in battle. Their images represented a two-dimensional reason for fighting for soldiers and sailors in precarious positions (Westbrook, 1990), serving as a reminder of what was, or could be, waiting for them back home. The positive and negative gravitas of the female role in hope-bringing is certainly an area worth further research.

Motion pictures had been previously used to stoke wartime sentiment (Fyne, 1994); Hollywood films provided a fresh canvas for propaganda to root and grow. Though *Casablanca* was "probably the most popular World War II film" (Fyne, 1994, p. 79), Walt Disney's animated shorts were incredibly popular. *The New Spirit* (1942), *Der Fuehrer's Face* (1943), and *Education for Death: The Making of the Nazi* (1943) were "government-sponsored films used to encourage Americans to pay their taxes . . . and encouraged support for America's effort and involvement in the war" (Cunningham, 2014, p. iii) while acknowledging the multifaceted fronts the United States was facing in both Europe and the Pacific.

The Rape of Nanking and the Bataan Death March provided a shifting theater for oppressors, victims, and observers (Murphy, 2011) with Pacific players. This setting provided a stark environment for art, a new reason to study the opposition, "to people at war after all, the major purpose in knowing one's enemies is to be better able to control or kill them" (Dower, 1987, p.

Figure 9.3. Bearded Man with Japanese Characters, created by an unknown artist at Manzanar, c. 1940s.

28). "The Japanese government was keenly aware of the importance of propaganda, especially film propaganda, in securing the support of the peoples" (Nieuwenhof, 1984, p. 161), a tactic they used to quickly inform Japanese citizens to continue support for what, at times, seemed like a hopeless cause. Indeed, psychological warfare was a determining factor of public opinion in World War II. Sometimes the wounds of the recent past were too fresh to shake, even during a new and different world war. For example, when the Australian Department of Information ran a two-week anti-Japanese campaign in the autumn of 1942, which included radio broadcasts detailing the brutal treatment of Australian prisoners of war in Japanese hands, they were flooded with protests from an Australian people who typically warned that Australians would not believe the type of stories that had turned out to be lies in WWI. (Finch, 2000, pp. 382–383)

The art of Australian World War II propaganda provides insight into Australia's shifting national identity and sometimes a fear of their "increasing dependence on the United States during the war" (Ozolins, 1993, p. 13). That sentiment, along with missed opportunities for increased communication and partnership via the Pacific War Council and the later-envisioned Pacific Advisory Commission, was lost after the death of Roosevelt (Kimball, 1994).

The Yalta Conference was followed by either Hitler's suicide or escape (Sognnaes, 1980) and Germany's surrender. This ultimately solidified the short and complicated relationship between Great Britain, the United States, and Russia that turned the combined forces of an unexpected alliance toward defeating Japan. The two atomic bombs were dropped at Hiroshima and Nagasaki, and Japan surrendered.

Japanese internment camps began closing in the United States in 1945; the last finally closed in 1946. That part of the story was over. But not really . . . an impression had been left, and for many, it has not faded. For many Japanese Americans, silence was and is the way to communicate the memory of the internment camp experience (Yamaguchi, 2014). "Individual differences in response to traumas vary depending on the circumstances but shared group experiences of historical and contemporary events can powerfully frame subsequent reactions and sense of well-being across time and generations" (Nagata et al., 2019, p. 46).

Generational considerations are often forgotten when we hear the story of history, which tends to lean toward the fantastic. For many texts, this is where the chapter ends because the war is over. But . . . what about war survivors? What about the survivors of Hiroshima and Nagasaki? Or those left in China after the Rape of Nanking?

What about children who survived the Holocaust? Various groups joined with the Youth Aliyah to help find child survivors and orphans of the Holocaust a new home and a new chance at life. For example, Mary Paneth, a former art therapist in London, met with eleven young women who were Holocaust survivors to draw and paint to help them cope with surviving, and with the memories they had of the experience (Hartsell, 2020). The gravitas of their work, an example of which is seen in figure 9.4, is difficult to describe in words, but it likely echoes the multifaceted experience of those whose story was not over yet . . . we need to remember to consider that when all the

118   Chapter Nine

Figure 9.4.   Painting by a Holocaust survivor.

bombing and diplomacy have subsided, there at the end, the story, our history, continues with the people who survived.

This chapter has discussed ways in which art was created by those experiencing hardship through the Great Depression and World War II. Impacts of social, political, and economic control and oppression as well as new innovations in art were reflected in pieces of the time. The suggested lessons in table 9.1, like the content of this chapter, is not exhaustive but instead serves as a foundation for your own exploration and inquiry. Please use these in the best way that works for you and your students.

Extend your lesson with these resources:

- Listen to Le Nom Cache, podcast, and the following synopsis by Duolingo: After his grandparents' deaths, twenty-year-old Damien Bouché uncovers a family secret from World War II. He spends the next ten years unearthing the past, from Vienna to the south of France, in a fight to regain his true family name. Part French/part English podcast, transcript available at the site: https://podcast.duolingo.com/episode-28-le-nom-cache-the-hidden-name.
- This panel discussed the moving story and the production of the film *The Windermere Children*, which brought to light the little-known history about the recovery and rehabilitation of three hundred young orphaned Jewish children who survived the Holocaust and were sent to the United Kingdom after the end of the Second World War. Watch here: http://webtv.un.org/search/discussion-of-the-film-%E2%80%9Cthe-windermere-children%E2%80%9D/6233327873001.

Table 9.1.

Warmup	Suggested activities	Closing
Lesson 1. Teacher pre-work: Explore the National World War II museum at https://www.nationalww2museum.org/students-teachers/educator-resources/classroom-resources to find a lesson that provides a cross-curricular focus. Warmup: Ask students, "Does social studies exist independently of other subjects? Why? Why not?" Allow time for students to discuss their answers.	• Conduct the cross-curricular lesson of your choice.	• Ask students to write a journal reflecting on their lesson experience today, specifically speaking to their impression of directed, cross-curricular learning.
Lesson 2. Teacher pre-work: Using documents and instructions from Doppen, F.H. (2000). Teaching and learning multiple perspectives: The atomic bomb. Social Studies, 91(4), 159–69. DOI: 10.1080/00377990009602461, create stations for students to read and investigate the documents provided in the article. Warmup: Ask students, "Are all consequences just good or just bad?" Allow students to share out and discuss.	• Allow students to explore the documents and files associated with the lesson. Then, using a human scale, explore the ideas of the article, allowing students to move as needed based on their changing opinions. Ask students to support their opinions with evidence from the texts—again, they may adjust their position throughout the activity.	• Quick write. Ask students to describe a circumstance that may have the same kinds of consequences they explored in today's lesson.
Lesson 3. Warmup: Ask students, "What does it mean to be a survivor?" Allow students to share out and discuss.	• Encourage students to get out their favorite art supplies, then invite them to explore the idea of being a survivor of World War II. Ask them to think of what event they would like to explore as a survivor as they create a visual art representation of what that identity is like.	• Closing: Ask students to display their survivor work with three hashtags that describe what their work conveys about the idea of surviving.

References

Barton, G.T., & Cooper, M.R. (1948). Relation of agricultural production to inputs. *Review of Economics and Statistics, 30*(2), 117–126.

Bohm-Duchen, M. (2014). *Art and the Second World War.* Princeton University Press.

Bresciani-Turroni, C. (2003). *The economics of inflation: A study of currency depreciation in post-war Germany, 1914–1923.* Routledge.

Chödrön, P. (2009, July 24). *Tonglen meditation.* Omega Institute for Holistic Studies. https://www.youtube.com/watch?v=QwqlurCvXuM.

Cole, M. (2021, December 31). Picasso and 'Guernica': Exploring the anti-war symbolism of this famous painting. *My Modern Met.*

Cunningham, A.M. (2014). *Walt Disney and the propaganda complex: Government funded animation and Hollywood complicity during WWII.* UNLV Theses, Dissertations, Professional Papers, and Capstones. 2072. http://dx.doi.org/10.34917/5836091.

Cushman, S. (2021, January 21). *Women and genocide.* United Nations Outreach Programme. https://media.un.org/en/asset/k11/k11c86nj18.

Dower, J. (1987). *War without mercy: Race and power in the Pacific War.* Pantheon.

Dusselier, J.E. (2005). Artful identifications: Crafting survival in Japanese American concentration camps. [Unpublished doctoral or master's thesis or dissertation]. University of Maryland.

Edmunds, R.D. (1995). Native Americans, new voices: American Indian history, 1895–1995. *The American Historical Review, 100*(3), 717–740.

Farnsworth, B. (2010). Conversing with Stalin, surviving the terror: The diaries of Aleksandra Kollontai and the internal life of politics. *Slavic Review, 69*(4), 944–970.

Federico, G. (2005). Not guilty? Agriculture in the 1920s and the Great Depression. *Journal of Economic History, 65*(4), 949–976.

Fein, H. (1979). *Accounting for genocide: Victims and survivors of the Holocaust.* Free Press.

Finch, L. (2000). Psychological propaganda: The war of ideas on ideas during the first half of the twentieth century. *Armed Forces & Society, 26*(3), 367–386.

Frank, A., & O'Brien, T. (2020). *The diary of a young girl.* New Central Book Agency.

Fyne, R. (1994). *The Hollywood propaganda of World War II.* Scarecrow Press.

Gellately, R., & Stolzfus, N. (2001). *Social outsiders in Nazi Germany.* Princeton University Press.

Gilad, E. (1 May 2019). Shoah: How a Biblical term became the Hebrew word for Holocaust. *Haaretz.*

Goeschel, C. (2018). *Mussolini and Hitler: The forging of the fascist alliance.* Yale University Press.

Green, J. (2013, October 10). *The Great Depression.* Crash Course.

Hacohen, D. (2001). British immigration policy to Palestine in the 1930s: Implications for Youth Aliyah. *Middle Eastern Studies, 37*(4), 206–218.

Harrer, H. (2007). *Beyond seven years in Tibet: My life before, during and after.* Labyrinth Press.

Hartsell, M. (2020, January 15). 'Lost Girls' artwork from the Holocaust. Library of Congress Blogs. https://blogs.loc.gov/loc/2020/01/lost-girls-artwork-from-the-holocaust/.

Hirsch, M. (2011). Mourning and postmemory. In Chaney, Michael A. (ed.). *Graphic subjects: critical essays on autobiography and graphic novels*. University of Wisconsin Press.

Houston, J.W., & Houston, J.D. (2017). *Farewell to manzanar*. Clarion Books.

Hurston, Z. (1937). *Their eyes were watching God*. Amistad.

Jachertz, R., & Nützenadel, A. (2011). Coping with hunger? Visions of a global food system, 1930–1960. *Journal of Global History, 6*(1), 99–119.

Kaltwasser, C.R., Taggart, P.A., Espejo, P.O., & Ostiguy, P. (2020). *The Oxford handbook of populism*. Oxford University Press.

Keen, K.H. (1980). Picasso's communist interlude: The murals of "war" and "peace." *Burlington Magazine, 122*(928), 464–470.

Kimball, W.F. (1994). "Merely a "açade"? Roosevelt and the southwest Pacific. *Journal of American-East Asian Relations, 3*(2), 103–126.

Langford, M. (2016). Migrant mothers: Richard Harrington's Indigenous 'Madonnas.' *History of Photography, 40*(1), 28–48.

Macciocchi, M.A. (1979). Female sexuality in fascist ideology. *Feminist Review, 1*, 67–82.

Meed, V. (1979). *On both sides of the wall: Memoirs from the Warsaw ghetto*. (Trans. Benjamin Meed). Holocaust Library.

Morison, S.E. (2001). *The rising sun in the Pacific, 1931–April 1942: History of United States Naval Operations in World War II, Vol. III*. University of Illinois Press.

Murphy, K. (2011). "To sympathize and exploit": Filipinos, Americans, and the Bataan Death March. *Journal of American-East Asian Relations, 18*(3–4), 295–319.

Nagata, D.K., Kim, J.H.J., & Wu, K. (2019). The Japanese American wartime incarceration: Examining the scope of racial trauma. *American Psychologist, 74*(1), 36–48.

Nieuwenhof, F. (1984). Japanese film propaganda in World War II: Indonesia and Australia. *Historical Journal of Film, Radio and Television, 4*(2), 161–177.

Okihiro, G.Y. (2005). *The Columbia guide to Asian American history*. Columbia University Press.

Ozolins, U. (1993). *The politics of language in Australia*. Cambridge University Press.

Preston, P. (2012). *The destruction of Guernica*. HarperCollins.

Richard, L. (1995). *L'art et la guerre: Les artistes confrontés à la Seconde guerre mondiale*. Flammarion.

Sims-Bishop, R. (1990). Mirrors, windows, and sliding glass doors. *Perspectives, 1*(3), ix–xi.

Snyder, T. (2010). *Bloodlands: Europe between Hitler and Stalin*. Basic Books.

Sognnaes, R.F., D.M.D., Ph.D. (1980). Hitler and Bormann identifications compared by postmortem craniofacial and dental characteristics. *American Journal of Forensic Medicine and Pathology, 1*(2), 105–116.

Spiegelman, A. (1996). *The complete Maus: A survivor's tale.* Pantheon Graphic Library.

Stackelberg, R., & Winkle, S.A. (2002). *The Nazi Germany sourcebook: An anthology of texts.* Routledge.

Takei, G., Eisinger, J., Scott, S., & Becker, H. (2019). *They called us enemy.* Top Shelf Productions.

Trigg, M. (2023). *Mothering, time, and antimaternalism: Motherhood under duress in the United States, 1920–1960.* Routledge.

Westbrook, R.B. (1990). "I want a girl, just like the girl that married Harry James": American women and the problem of political obligation in World War II. *American Quarterly, 42*(4), 587–614.

Yamaguchi, P. (2014). *Experiences of Japanese American women during and after World War II: Living in internment camps and rebuilding life afterwards.* Lexington Books.

Chapter Ten

Frozen Remix: Navigating the Cold War

Navigating the Cold War 1945–1991

Scholars sometimes enjoy a good debate, and determining whether the Cold War started during World War II is one of many that continue regarding political science and diplomacy. The Iron Curtain speech piqued the interest of many citizens of the West because they had continued to view the Soviet Union as a kind of ally after the defeat of Nazi Germany (Young & Kent, 2020). Buffer zones surrounded increasingly polar spheres of influence as the United States and the USSR grappled for global hegemony. Instead of a "hot" World War III built from the ashes of the first two, the world found itself frozen.

Suggestions for mindfulness aligned to this content are adapted from Gandhi's reflections on finding unity in things (Ghandi, 1971). As you are interacting with the content of this chapter, consider the following questions:

- Where do you find unity in the experiences of the people living through the time of the Cold War?
- When do you have thoughts of conflict regarding unity and disunity as you explore this chapter?
- What methods can you use to center your thoughts and breath to help you stretch through conflicting ideas and into ideas of unity?

GUIDING QUESTIONS

- How did the Cold War change the way in which nationalism was expressed in art?
- How did art of the Cold War express the changing perceptions of the roles of people in a society?
- How did art reflect the changes in international diplomacy during the Cold War?

The start of the Greek Civil War among other political actions, including the Iron Curtain speech, solidified a new way of diplomacy. "The Truman Doctrine . . . is generally accepted as the real beginning of the Cold War; at least it is the declaration of full American involvement" (Frazier, 1984, p. 715), and in partnership with the United Kingdom, the United States began aggressive containment initiatives. Countries like Poland, Turkey, Greece, and Iran shifted, often violently, to communism. The desperation to prevent the domino theory from becoming a reality hit a fever pitch with counter political moves like the Berlin Airlift, the Treaty of Washington, and the creation of NATO, a jockeying of capitalist allies to save their position, and to persuade others to join.

China remained in a liminal space regarding diplomacy and political leadership that in many ways continued feelings of uncertainty. These feelings had been in place since the conclusion of the Opium Wars, which left extraterritoriality and the ownership of Shanghai on the table for foreigners, particularly the British. The civil war in 1911 left uncertainties regarding the status of China as pro-communist with leadership in Nationalists rising in efforts to reunify the Middle Kingdom. However, the communist revolution in 1949, and the subsequent Great Leap Forward, solidified China as communist. The Chinese (forced) annexation of Tibet, Taiwan, and the Hainan Island (Shakya, 1999, p. 3) led to mixed messages being sent to citizens, like what is seen in figure 10.1.

Figure 10.1. Chinese and Tibetan government officials at a banquet celebrating the "peaceful liberation" of Tibet, photographer unknown, taken 1951.

Here there are people wearing dignified clothing, appearing to have some semblance of cooperation and unity, but there is an uncertainty about the validity of that message being sent, particularly with the exile of the Dalai Lama, among other acts on part of the newly founded People's Republic of China that intensified fears of the communist fall of Japan, a newly renovated economic hub.

Italian fascist cells had begun to swell in the early 1920s internationally (de Caprariis, 2000) because of the vacuum of Mussolini's power. But by the early 1930s, they had "lost all significance" (de Caprariis, 2000, p. 183); still, remaining Italian immigrant feelings of nationalism (Beals, 1938) made South America ripe for the reemergence of fascism. South American investments in World War II were closely tied to the economy; for example, "Argentina supplied 40% of British meat during WWII" (Green, 2012). After the conclusion of the war, those remaining preconditions, along with German Nazi immigrants (Hevia Jordán, 2022), provided further justification for fascism to reemerge after World War II in Argentina, Bolivia, Brazil, Chile, Columbia, Ecuador, Paraguay, Peru, Uruguay, and Venezuela.

Juan Peron, the president of Argentina, admired Mussolini (Eatwell & Wright, 1999, p. 196) and Hitler (Pigna, 2008, p. 28). Peron and his second wife, Eva, attempted to eliminate poverty and uplift hard work and the common man, even as they welcomed "some of the worst Nazi criminals and collaborators" to Argentina (Goñi, 2022, p. 157). Eva Peron was celebrated throughout her country for a multitude of reasons. The imagery and collective Argentinian memory associated with Eva paints her literally and figuratively as a modern-day Cinderella, as seen in figure 10.2. Although Eva "has never been implicated in her husband's rumored activities with Nazi war criminals" (Allison, 2004, p. 23), she stood by his side for eight years. Throughout Juan's rise to power and campaigning, Eva also petitioned for women's suffrage and conducted other charitable acts, even as "Argentina was a Nazi haven" (Allison, 2004, p. 24).

Because of new rips in old wounds made fresh by a sustained Nazi presence in the aftermath of World War II, artists like Walt Disney continued working on projects sponsored by the United States government. Disney and his team were hired to create the "good neighbor" films *Saludos Amigos* and *The Three Caballeros* to try to deter Nazi efforts in Latin America. These films intentionally fused cartoons and real-life images to engage audiences of both adults and children. Many artists joined the effort to help contextualize happenings in a way that made sense to youngsters. For example, Dr. Seuss intentionally wrote children's books with deeply relevant socio-cultural themes in a way that children could understand, in his words, "to attack what I think are evil things" (Cott, 1984, p. 30) while promoting positive social behaviors. As the Cold War frosted on,

Figure 10.2. Retrato del Presidente Juan Domingo Perón y su señora esposa María Eva Duarte de Perón, painted by Numa Ayrinhac c. 1948.

the exaggerated threat of communist "atom spies," in addition to a real Soviet-American crisis in Iran, produced the necessary psychological justification for gathering public support . . . and also provided the backdrop against which the Truman administration evolved its long-term strategy for countering Soviet communism. (Herken, 1988, p. 136)

The Cold War was not limited to weapons, but also to abstractions. Suspicions rose along with McCarthyism; the Kitchen Debates also added another dimension to the juxtapositions of the conflict, and media continually fanned the already-roaring flames of suspicion in sometimes comical ways (see figure 10.3).

Slippery transitions of power after Eva Peron's death and Juan's struggle to maintain authority led to a coup and later the Dirty War, which was "no real war, but instead the state sanctioned mass killings of citizens" in Argentina

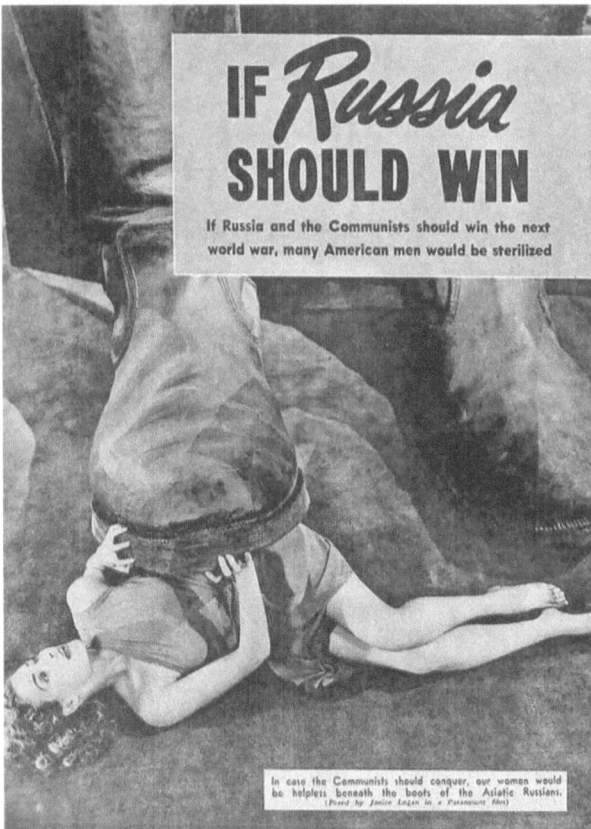

Figure 10.3. If Russia Should Win, visual art by *Man to Man* magazine, January 1954.

(Finchelstein, 2014, p. 162). Similar coups occurred in Chile, where Augusto Pinochet supported the Colonia Dignidad, another Nazi resettlement (Infield, 1990). Despite being a neofascist (Bosworth, 2009, p. 604), Pinochet was an anti-communist, a detail that kept his image a quarter turn away from being known only as pro-Nazi.

The hot parts of the Cold War included the Korean War, Vietnam War, and the Cuban missile crisis. These impacted families in the United States and abroad, but there were also very real cultural wars happening, sometimes in much closer contexts to citizens' everyday lives. For example, the launching of Sputnik led to a fear of United States schools underperforming against Soviet educational systems, and so began the era of standardized testing (Addison & McGee, 2015). The newly established National Aeronautics and Space Administration (NASA) in the United States and Soviet space programs raced for hegemony not only on Earth, but also in space.

Again, art was impacted by these leaps into the unknown. Even with the rise of television shows, "situation comedies" or "sitcoms" rose in popularity in the 1950s (Dalton & Linder, 2012). Shows like *I Dream of Jeannie* and later *M*A*S*H** provided a spectrum of perspectives—some realistic, others fantastical—for viewers who might have been trying to process or find connection with others through curiosity or memories of the past and sometimes the present. Again, producers found ways to integrate children into television experiences. *The Smurfs* originally aired in Belgium in the 1970s, but the show came to the United States in 1981 with strong communist undertones, and "while no data is available directly for communist propaganda, there is an impression that some details are selected ideologically and presented positively" (Ağırseven & Örki, 2017, p. 844). Some say the diverse but cooperative, capitalist Snorks were brought about to try to turn around any pro-communist ideations that might have bubbled up in children from watching the Smurfs.

Unintended consequences call for teamwork, reciprocity, and cooperation in order for reconciliation to occur. The ending of the Cold War required just that. Leadership from social, political, and economic factions worked together to find ways to collapse communism that sometimes happened peacefully, others forcefully. The Cold War unwound in pieces. China's command economy grew, and with it, a Chinese presence in the global economy. Soviet leader Mikhail Gorbachev and his policies of glasnost and perestroika allowed for the gradual opening and eventual unraveling of the Soviet Union. The Berlin Wall fell in a symbolic beginning of the end of conflict (Freedman, 2002), and by late 1991, the Cold War was over. Still, its lasting effects provide a firm tapestry of which we are still very much a part in today's world.

This chapter has discussed ways in which people living through the Cold War experienced unity, or similar fears and hopes in their lives. The content explored ways in which nationalism was expressed directly and indirectly in the arts, as well as how the arts embodied a changing understanding of the roles of people in society. Additionally suggested artful expressions helped illustrate ways in which international diplomacy changed during the Cold War. Suggested lesson plans are in table 10.1; please use these to find what works best for you and for your students.

Extend the lesson with these resources:

- Listen to *Comment je m'appelle*, a podcast and the following synopsis by Duolingo: Growing up in France, Hong Dagognet rarely spoke with her adoptive parents about her childhood in Vietnam. But after receiving a surprising letter, she set out to reconnect with her family and finally unveil the mysteries of her past. Part French/part English podcast, transcript available at the website: https://podcast.duolingo.com/episode-8-comment-je-mappelle-whats-my-name.
- Find and watch the *Penguins of Madagascar* episode that addresses McCarthyism: "The Red Squirrel" (season 2, episode 1). Have a discussion that compares what happened in the episode to what happened in real life in the United States. Finally, as a class, consider whether it is important for cartoons and other forms of media (like movies) to bring up serious issues framed in a way that works for kids. Why? Why not?
- Print off and compare Billy Joel's 1989 "We Didn't Start the Fire" with Fall Out Boy's 2023 "We Didn't Start the Fire." Note what kinds of issues were consistent between the two, and which were different.

Table 10.1.

Warmup	Suggested activities	Closing
Lesson 1. Warmup: Ask students to identify TWO origins of the Cold War. After they have a chance to respond to that, ask them to share out and compare their answers, looking at the differences of their responses and then deciding which two are most important.	• Activity: Today students will participate in a Socratic seminar activity with one leader acting as "Socrates" to pose the following questions for discussion. Encourage students to use evidence from their findings in the chapter to support their responses. Finally, remember that thoughtful discussion takes time, so it's okay to pause and reflect for a time. • Why is it called the "Cold War"? • What do you think it means for a conflict to become a "hot" war? • Which is more dangerous? Why? • Can an individual make a difference in a global conflict? Why? Why not?	• Parking lot: Students will do a quick write on a Post-it Note that they will "park" on the door as they are leaving, identifying and explaining what they thought the most important part of today's discussion was for them as citizens and as humans. • NOTE: Collect and use these parking lot responses as you begin the discussion in tomorrow's warmup.
Lesson 2. Ask students, "How do you know when an event has ended?" Have them share out and discuss. Then expand the conversation by asking, "How do you know when a war is ended? Would you know when a war has ended first as a citizen or as a human? Is there a difference in those identities? Why? Why not?"	• Choose one country or region that was a part of the Cold War. Then ask students to reflect on how that country or region knew the Cold War was over and the impact that the war concluding had on their daily lives. • Extend the activity: Research the life of Ho Van Lang. Discuss whether you think there may be others like him still alive—where would they be? You may also choose to research other incidents like this that have occurred through time.	• Turn and talk. Some historians and cultural anthropologists contend that the Cold War is still not over. Ask students what they think about this claim and why or why they do not support it using evidence in their stance.
Lesson 3. Warmup: Assign students to read this article from Rolling Stone about the origin of the Billy Joel song, "We Didn't Start the Fire." Note: you should consider reading this first and making necessary modifications to accommodate different readers in your class. See https://www.rollingstone.com/music-news/we-didnt-start-the-fire-billy-joel-history-926129/.	• Discuss the article: Why was the song written? What was Joel trying to convey to his audience through this work? • Activity: Randomly assign students a line or lines from "We Didn't Start the Fire," then ask them to research what the line was about and why they think it was important to include in the song. Then ask students to do a quick write comparing that lyric/event/person to something they have already learned about in class or something they are learning about in today's current events. Share out or post student work.	• Quick write. Ask students to create a three-to-five-song playlist that captures what else they think should be expressed or enriched in order to know more about the Cold War. Their writing should include song titles, artists (if possible), and an explanation of how those songs help enrich the story of the Cold War when paired with "We Didn't Start the Fire."

References

Addison, J. & McGee, S.J. (2015). To the core: College composition classrooms in the age of accountability, standardized testing, and Common Core state standards. *Rhetoric Review, 34*(2), 200–218.

Ağırseven, N., & Örki, A. (2017). Evaluating Turkish TV series as soft power instruments. *International Journal of Society Researches, 7*(13), 838–853.

Allison, V. (2004). White evil: Peronist Argentina in the US popular imagination since 1955. *American Studies International, 42*(1), 4–48.

Beals, C. (1938). Black shirts in Latin America. *Current History (1916–1940), 49*(3), 32–34.

Bosworth, R.J.B. (2009). *The Oxford handbook of fascism*. Oxford University Press.

Cott, J. (1984). *Pipers at the gates of dawn: The wisdom of children's literature*. McGraw-Hill.

Dalton, M.M., & Linder, L.R. (2012). *The sitcom reader: America viewed and skewed*. State University of New York Press.

de Caprariis, L. (2000). 'Fascism for export'? The rise and eclipse of the fasci Italiani all'estero. *Journal of Contemporary History, 35*(2), 151–183.

Eatwell, R., & Wright, A. (1999). *Contemporary political ideologies*. Continuum.

Felipe, P. (2008). *Mitos de la historia Argentina 4*. Planeta.

Finchelstein, F. (2014). *The ideological origins of the Dirty War: Fascism, populism, and dictatorship in twentieth century Argentina*. Oxford University Press.

Frazier, R. (1984). Did Britain start the Cold War? Bevin and the Truman Doctrine. *Historical Journal, 27*(3), 715–727.

Freedman, L. (2002). Berlin and the Cold War. In: Gearson, J.P.S., Schake, K. (eds) *The Berlin Wall Crisis*. Cold War History Series. Palgrave Macmillan.

Ghandi, M. (1971). *All men are brothers: Life and thoughts of Mahatma Gandhi as told in his own words*. Navajivan Publishing House.

Goñi, U. (2022). *The real Odessa: How Perón brought the Nazi war criminals to Argentina*. Granta Books.

Green, J. (2012, October 11). *World War II*. Crash Course.

Herken, G. (1988). *The winning weapon: The atomic bomb in the Cold War, 1945–1950*. Princeton University Press.

Hevia Jordán, E. (2022). Colonia dignidad: Lights and shadows in the recognition of the victims. In Elizabeth Lira; Marcela Cornejo; Germán Morales (eds.). *Human rights violations in Latin America: Reparation and rehabilitation* (pp. 223–236). Springer International Publishing.

Infield, G.B. (1990). *Secrets of the ss*. Jove.

Shakya, T. (1999). *The dragon in the land of snows: A history of modern Tibet since 1947*. Penguin Books.

Young, J.W. & Kent, J. (2020). *International relations since 1945: A global history (3rd ed.)*. Oxford: Oxford University Press.

Chapter Eleven

Am I Wrong for Thinkin' Out the Box from Where I Stay?

New Identities, Decolonization, Revolutions, and Revolutionary Impacts Circa 1950–2023

It is notable that this chapter is often presented at the end of the instructional cycle, or the end of the text, as it is here because this content often lends itself to exploration and action. It also lends itself to uncertainty; this is where content and the now intersect. Some think the script for the now is already written, that not only is the present stuck in a time of transition, but also that it indicates a continual clash of civilizations (Jones, 2001). Indeed, clashes, identities, continuing conflict, violence . . . those realities still exist, but there is always a choice to reach for something new and different in the future.

Suggestions for mindfulness aligned to this content, adapted from the National Mass Violence Victimization Resource Center (2021, p. 1), are based on the idea that you do not have to walk away from normal activities to find a space for mindfulness, but that mindfulness can be achieved through simple activities with purpose and without judgment. Some ideas include:

- Listening to music fully, without thinking about other things.
- Making a cup of tea or coffee and slowly enjoying it.
- Exercising with intention and focus.
- Walking and noticing the world around you.
- Eating mindfully, taking time to really taste the food.
- Stepping outside to be outdoors and/or in nature.
- Listening and reflecting while in a conversation with someone else.

GUIDING QUESTIONS

- How did art provide a medium for expressing the socio-cultural revolutions of the twentieth and twenty-first centuries?

- How has art been used to frame awareness and advocacy in the twentieth and twenty-first centuries?
- How does art support ideas of informed action in the twentieth and twenty-first centuries?

World War II left innumerable scars on the collective consciousness, but one somewhat productive, not new, but newly acknowledged way of thinking was a rejection of imperialism, caused by a global majority disliking Hitler and his Nazi movement. However, colonies demanding independence sometimes lacked infrastructure and other constructs that they might have come to rely on from colonial powers. Furthermore, the idea of (the Western definition of) national identity became complicated for those in newly independent former colonies who sought ways to find dignity, identity, and power in the modern age.

Identity is tied into many things, including foods, and with that, the harvest and methods of farming. The Green Revolution, also known as the Third Agricultural Revolution, started in Mexico in 1943. Mexico was in many ways still recovering from the Mexican Revolution (1910–1920) at the time, and that coincided with other, complicated global issues, including the Zimmerman telegram (1917), and other local issues that many Latin American countries were facing as the hacienda system became abandoned, leaving many people without land and demanding land redistribution.

The Green Revolution provided a solution to that and was supported by Mexican president Manual Avila Camacho in partnership with the United States government, the United Nations Food and Agriculture Organization, and others in hopes of providing food relief for an increasing populace. To achieve that goal, initiatives first focused on ideas centering on food production, but "farming is not the same everywhere, and it does not always present the same face to the world" (McGregor, 2015, p. 297). It goes without saying the Green Revolution had mixed results and mixed responses from global citizens. Have you ever thought about where the food you eat comes from or how it is harvested and grown? Is there a cultural resonance in that cultivation? Why? Why not? These are important considerations; after all, the saying, "if you eat today, thank a farmer," is not without merit.

Finding and claiming modern identity in statehood can sometimes be dangerous, like in the case of genocide. For example, the earlier Armenian genocide, the continued genocide of Native Americans/Indigenous people, the Silent Holocaust of the Mayans, and the genocide of the Uyghurs provide stark perspectives on what danger lies in the search for a state-based identity. That scarring, and the art that has been produced because of it, is certainly another avenue to explore independently and mindfully.

Identity can also be shaped by an anti-colonial mindset. When Charles deGaulle made his speech in Constantine, Algeria, in October 1958, he outlined a gradual release model of leadership and politicization to aid Algeria and other former colonies while inviting Algerians and others to still identify as French citizens; this sentiment had mixed responses. Citizens in former colonies, even today, struggle with (or embrace) what many see as a complex identity because notions of nationalism are, by and large, a Western construct, while tribal associations are in some cases more valuable and more culturally appropriate for the people in particular areas or regions.

Struggles with identity have risen as evidence of the difficulties emerging with decolonization, particularly in sub-Saharan Africa. Here, "precolonial statehood has contributed to political violence in Africa," like the Rwandan genocide, and "non-pre-colonial states have experienced more civil wars as new cleavages emerged after the Soviet Union fell" (Paine, 2019, p. 679). This speaks not only to identity complexity in the decolonized world, but also to fragile ways of self-identifying in pre-colonized times. In the same vein of thought, art pieces such as the *African Renaissance Monument*, found in figure 11.1, provide perspectives on liberation, reclaiming, and empowering citizens. The idea for this structure was created to celebrate liberation and empowerment; the statue was unveiled after Senegal's fiftieth anniversary of liberation from France.

Figure 11.1. African Renaissance Monument, statue designed by Senegalese architect Pierre Goudiaby based on an idea presented by President Abdoulaye Wade and built by Mansudae Overseas Projects, 2010.

Films like *Blood Diamond* speak to direct issues impacting post-colonial sub-Saharan Africa. The Sierra Leonian Civil War provided a backdrop for this film's call to viewers' attention, and hopefully action, regarding the diamond industry. Other films like *District 9* indirectly address real-life issues like apartheid through fictional storytelling (deWaal, 2009). The continued success of Marvel's *Black Panther* films speaks to the diversity of African cultures, while providing a foundation for Afro-futurism in media, a way to disrupt narratives and provide a new hope for the future (Boyd Acuff, 2020).

The Islamicate has reclaimed power through transnational anti-colonial movements in places like Egypt, India (Gani, 2023), and other parts of the Middle East and North Africa. The Iranian Islamic Revolution of the late 1970s "extended beyond geographical, lingual, and sectarian boundaries" (Thodika, 2023, p. 8). Marjane Satrapi provides a window to peer inside what the revolution was like for her between the ages of six to fourteen in her graphic novel, *Persepolis* (2004). Youth have an increasingly important role in cultivating change, which can sometimes be dangerous. Take the Arab Spring, a movement that "should be examined as an expression of a powerful socio-cultural frustration: the inability of youth to achieve adulthood, held back by governments and markets that stall youth engagement" (Mulderig, 2013, p. 3) in Egypt, Libya, Syria, Bahrain, Tunisia, and Yemen.

The "2011 Egyptian Revolution," in particular, illustrates "how social media catalyzes social change across different phases including the initial formation of communities, as well as the promotion of a coordinated movement" (Fakhry et al., 2023, p. 7); more broadly, the Arab Spring showed the power of social media (Mellen, 2012) and the impact of globalization. Something to consider: many argue that events like the Arab Spring provide support for the idea that the internet has democratized knowledge, while others posit that freedom of expression should not mean unlimited freedom in the effort to maintain global digital democracy (Congee, 2023). What do you think?

The technology revolution is not limited to social media; there are also long-term impacts of nuclear arms building and the use of nuclear power. Scientists are continuing explorations of renewable energy sources and ways to remediate loss of green space. Concern about environmental change and the impact of human interaction on that is not new. For example, scientists are continuing to explore and find new ways of farming, including ways to restore and reinvent forests through the creation and maintenance of urban forests like the Tijuca Forest in the Tijuca National Park. Reforestation of the area began as early as the late nineteenth century, as seen in figure 11.2.

This captures the idea that reforestation and the importance of trees was acknowledged by politicians, even then. The Tijuca Forest formally became a National Park in 1961 and a UNESCO World Heritage Site in 2012,

Figure 11.2. The Chinese View of Tijuca: Tijuca Forest, photographed by George Leuzinger c. 1865-1874.

solidifying its importance in today's world not only as a tourist site but as a place to reclaim land for the environment.

There is also an increasing concern for ocean health, including a concern for rising sea levels, as seen in figure 11.3. Carbon footprint considerations are now printed on products from water bottles to airplane tickets. There is also an implied carbon footprint present when shoppers choose to buy local foods and other goods versus outsourced items from other localities. The impact of choices about food, clothing, other products, and even travel is evident in the environmental costs of those purchases. Artists again have risen to the challenge of addressing these issues through films that directly address environmental worry, like *I am Greta*, *An Inconvenient Truth*, *An Inconvenient Sequel: Truth to Power*, and *Our Great National Parks*. Some filmmakers choose to create indirect environmental stories like *WALL-E*, *FernGully*, and *Captain Planet* to spark curiosity and inspire informed action. Musicians have also voiced concern for environmental advocacy (i.e., Xiuhtezcatl Martinez, Paul McCartney, Childish Gambino, Billie Eilish, Neil Young, Foals, Lana Del Rey, The Climate Music Project, Bon Iver, and Grimes).

Figure 11.3. Support, sculpture by Lorenzo Quinn, 2017.

Indirect artful expression in today's world sometimes provides a clearer window into reality than previously seen. For example, former Tehranian journalist Masih Alinejad attested that not only is the fictional piece *A Handmaid's Tale* happening today in Iran, but that the leaders there kicked her out for using her voice: "They're scared of my words, they're scared of my voice" (2022). Similar strife is felt by women in the United States; the film *An Amish Sin* points a spotlight on women being abused in its Amish communities. Multi-talented global artists Shakira and Jennifer Lopez used their performance at the Super Bowl as a platform not only to incorporate Latinidad, but also to inform (and hopefully inspire activism) about children being held in cages. This performance showed the power that intersectionality—in this case, music, dance, and political outcry—can have when presented at a popular sporting event in a performance art form that is televised (Van Bauwel & Krijnen, 2021).

Concerns for women's and children's rights are ongoing, and they continue to be centered during times of global crisis:

> the Covid pandemic has highlighted this issue by exacerbating the vulnerability of that group, even if the virus doesn't discriminate, women and girls have been impacted the most through sexual violence and domestic violence during the lockdown . . . Women are in more frontline jobs, being more exposed to the virus, and their productive and economic lives have been more profoundly impacted by the Pandemic than men. (Cruciani, 2021)

Perhaps the most that can be gained from that information is that there continues to be opportunity for growth; that as global citizens, awareness, advocacy, and community can not only empower, but that they, and taking informed action, can also save lives. Even in stark moments of harsh realities, there is hope in art. A study on themes found that in Paris and Milan's destination marketing organizations (DMOs) during the lockdown part of the COVID-19 pandemic, visual themes, such as promoting safety, promoting pro-social behaviors, and reopening information, kept citizens engaged and provided avenues for hope. Andrea Bocelli's livestreamed "Music for Hope" performance on YouTube in April 2020 is another example of a celebrity using his voice to connect, strengthen, and unify the global community, who were in a time of crisis.

This chapter has discussed ways in which art provided a medium for expression for revolution, awareness, and advocacy as well as informed action in the twentieth and twenty-first centuries. The mindfulness activity for this chapter encouraged readers to find moments of mindfulness in their day, experiencing them with intention to be more in the now and in the self. Finally, you will see there are lesson suggestions in table 11.1; please use or modify these to meet the needs of your students.

Extend the lesson.

- Watch *Nuclear Boy* on YouTube, a video created to explain what happened at Fukushima to children; see https://www.youtube.com/watch?v=5sakN2hSVxA; have a class discussion on what students think of the video—does it have the potential to help or harm? Why?

Table 11.1.

Warmup	Suggested activities	Closing
Lesson 1. Ask students, "What role do you think global conflict had in bringing about independence movements?" Have them share out and discuss. Then expand the conversation by asking, "How do you think people would feel about their citizenship if they were citizens in a colony that had not yet gained independence?"	• First, students will choose a conflict from the module to use in their research to find ways that diplomacy was maintained or changed during the conflict they chose. • Then, students will create a visual-art presentation explaining how the effects of independence movements in the region they chose are still a part of life today. • Finally, students will share out, post, or present their findings, looking for similarities in experiences.	• Exit ticket: Students will do a quick write comparing and contrasting life in two newly independent regions.
Lesson 2. Ask students, "Does a bartering system have a place in today's world? Why? Why not?" Allow time for consideration and discussion.	• Today students will research how modern economic movements have been impacted by new ideas about currency. Students will then create the story of their own nation, deciding what kind of social, political, economic, environmental, and demographic variables will be a part of their new nation. What would be the benefits of the new nation? • Assessment: Students will create a two-to five-minute commercial persuading others to come to live in their nation.	• Quick write: How could the experience of creating your own nation translate into what you do in your life in the next year? What about the next ten years?
Lesson 3. Ask students, "How do environmental issues impact our social and political lives?" Allow students to share out and discuss. Expand the conversation by asking, "How do climate-change issues relate to issues of equity and justice?" Again, allow time for discussion.	• Students will divide into flexible groups to identify an environmental issue in today's world. Then they will create something with found/repurposed materials that explains a solution(s) to the problem they identified. • Each group will have the chance to present, and then the class will discuss the proposals.	• Turn and talk. Ask students if any, some, or all these solutions could lead to informed action; then have them share their thoughts on a "parking lot" post it to close.

References

Boyd Acuff, J. (2020). Afrofuturism: Reimagining art curricula for Black existence. *Art Education, 73*(3), 13–21.

Congge, U., Guillamón, M.D., Nurmandi, A., Salahudin, S., & Salahudin, S.I.T. (2023). Digital democracy: A systematic literature review. *Frontiers in Political Science, 5*(972802), 1–11.

Cruciani, S. (2021, January 21). *Women and genocide*. United Nations Outreach Programme. https://media.un.org/en/asset/k11/k11c86nj18.

de Waal, Shaun. (28 August 2009). Loving the aliens. *Mail & Guardian*. https://mg.co.za/article/2009-08-28-loving-the-aliens/.

Droney, D. (2021). In the path of the Black Panther: Science, technology, and speculative fiction in African studies. *KNOW: A Journal on the Formation of Knowledge, 5*(1), 27–52.

Fakhry, B., Tarabasz, A., & Selakovic, M. (2023). Social media & uprisings: The case of the Egyptian revolution in 2011. *MATEC Web Conference, 377*(2023), 1–10.

Gani, J.K. (2023). Anti-colonial connectivity between Islamicate movements in the Middle East and South Asia: The Muslim Brotherhood and Jamati Islam. *Postcolonial Studies, 26*(1), 55–76.

Hoover, M., (Host, *The Firing Line with Margaret Hoover*) & Masih Alinejad. (2022, October 14). *The Firing Line with Margaret Hoover*. Kera Network, Dallas. Retrieved from https://www.pbs.org/wnet/firing-line/video/masih-alinejad-0sf2x6/.

Jones, A. (2001, October 26). Memories of crusades live on in today's war. *National Catholic Reporter*.

McGregor, J.H. (2015). *Back to the Garden. Nature and the Mediterranean world from prehistory to the present*. Yale University Press.

Mellen, R. (2012). Modern Arab uprisings and social media: An historical perspective on media and revolution. *Explorations in Media Ecology, 11*(2), 115–130.

Mulderig, M.C. (2013, April). An uncertain future: Youth frustration and the Arab Spring. *Pardee Papers, 16*, 1–26.

National Mass Violence Victimization Resource Center. (2021). *Mindfulness and meditation to support resilience after mass violence*. National Mass Violence Victimization Resource Center Department of Psychiatry and Behavioral Sciences Medical University of South Carolina.

Paine, J. (2019). Ethnic violence in Africa: Destructive legacies of pre-colonial states. *International Organization, 73*(3), 645–683.

Thodika, S.K. (2023). Iranian Islamic Revolution and the transformation of Islamist discourse in Southern India: 1979–1992. *Religions, 14*(130), 1–10.

Van Bauwel, S., & Krijnen, T. (2021). Let's get loud: Intersectionally studying the Super Bowl's halftime show. *Media and Communication, 9*(2), 209–217.

Conclusion

We Are the People We've Been Waiting For

> There is an ancient Indian saying that something lives only as long as the last person who remembers it. My people have come to trust memory over history. Memory, like fire, is radiant and immutable while history serves only those who seek to control it, those who douse the flame of memory in order to put out the dangerous fire of truth. Beware these men for they are dangerous themselves and unwise. Their false history is written in the blood of those who might remember and of those who seek the truth.
>
> (Carter, 1995)

Maybe that is why we must look at art . . . because art is wild. Art is where people have stored their stories and memories for longer than they were able to express such things in written words. I'm not sure if the person who wrote that episode of *X-Files* you see quoted above was Indigenous, but the intent of the writer is evident: that we should seek the truth; that we should look deeper and consider stories and tradition as we imagine the past.

One goal of this text was to challenge you to look beyond art as it is, practicing mindfulness and empathy to examine the art, looking to gain a more enriched understanding of humanity, continuing to actively seek that connection, and then passing that practice on to your students—because "time, history, and the future is complex" (Cregan-Reid, 2015, p. 210). As educators, we know that we are unceasingly faced with that complexity.

After all, we are humans communicating with and teaching other humans about humans—our work as educators places us knowingly in that hall of mirrors where we have to check in with ourselves personally and professionally before entering the classroom every day. We ask ourselves, "Am I okay? What content could be triggering today for myself or my students? How can

I support and grow through those emotions with my students and model for them what that looks like independently?" We have conversations in our classrooms—hard conversations; necessary conversations about humanity and its flaws—and yet we continue to stretch ourselves and our students into that challenge in the hope of co-constructing a better tomorrow. Someone has to take the first step. The first step is examining the art, the issue, the calamity, the person. The next step is stretching into mindfulness, remembering that these factors are not variables that we invented, but the imprint of our collective past. In step three, we need to talk about things. We need to talk about what happened and discuss what our students think, feel, or see, and then unpack the "so what" factor. We have to allow for dialogue, and that is, in many ways, absolutely terrifying. We never know what our students will say or how the conversation will go, but we know that no matter what, that kind of exchange is critical in order for students to grow as scholars, as citizens, and as people.

> By providing curricular contexts that model respectful and thoughtful exchange and by helping youth think more fully about the ways others may hear what they say, educators can help young people develop both the skills and the desire to exercise their speech rights in ways that advance a diverse society and foster a healthier and more inclusive democracy. (Kahne & Cortes, 2023, p. 20)

By allowing and encouraging students to think, reflect, and speak, we are empowering them with the experience of what freedom of speech looks like in practice and how it can be difficult to navigate, but also that it is vital to our classroom, just as it is in society. Ultimately schools are small representations of the communities in which they are located (Haupt, 2010; Levesque, & Croteau, 2022), so imagine the long-term impact we could have as educators if we continue to model the freedom to think, speak, and take informed action.

This text provided strategies to implement mindfulness practices into your reading and interpretation of the text. Mindfulness practices included offerings from Thích Nhất Hạnh, Pema Chödrön, and others who have dedicated their lives to mindfulness practice and to bringing that state of being to others. There were fragments of some stories sprinkled throughout; these were shared with the hope of inspiring further avenues for an independent, mindful historical exploration after this text is closed. There were also lesson plan suggestions that outlined ways to create pathways to bring this content to your students with flexibility and adaptations suggested along with encouragement to spark your own creativity.

I encourage you to actively seek out stories that show students good examples of humanity. There are so many instances of unity that are being centered, and those are the stories that I hope will continue to be elevated.

For example, when Iran was eliminated from the World Cup in 2022, the United States Men's team comforted their players. When asked why, one of the American players, Tim Weah, said:

> I just wanted to show that we are all human beings and we all love each other. I just wanted to spread peace and love and show him we come from different backgrounds, we grew up differently. He is still my family, he is still my brother, and I love him the same way as the guys I grew up with. (Rogers, 2022)

Those are the stories our students need to hear. Yes, we need to speak the truth, and the truth of our collective past, because that holds power. We also need to find places, experiences, and ways that unite us if we are going to make a positive impact moving forward.

The COVID-19 pandemic and subsequent lockdown brought about a series of events that imprinted on the lives of people around the globe in different ways. Teachers need additional training on social and emotional learning strategies to use in their classrooms, and students need more of those experiences to enrich their lives at school and their personal development (Jennings & Min, 2023). This text has reached toward that goal of providing a foundation to grow from with stories, art, mindfulness experiences, and lesson plans that center social and emotional considerations while supplementing content-based learning.

As we continue to emerge from the aftermath of that experience, Bill and Ted posed an observation that "sometimes things don't make sense, until the end of the story" (2021). I tend to agree with Bill and Ted on most things, but I'm not sure we will ever make sense of the story of us, and I'm not sure that finding sense in the story is what really matters. What I do know is this: we are teachers, and we are here for the hard reset (Ladson-Billings, 2021). By exploring humanity through art and storytelling, through practicing mindfulness and compassion for ourselves and others, we can make positive changes in the world one student at a time—and that is what matters.

References

Carter, C.C. (Writer), & Goodwin, R.W. (Director). (1995). The blessing way [Television series episode]. In C.C. Carter (Producer), *The X-Files*. North Vancouver, British Columbia, Canada: 20th Century Fox Television.

Cregan-Reid, V. (2015). *Discovering Gilgamesh: Geology, narrative and the historical sublime in Victorian culture*. Manchester University Press.

Haupt, P.M. (2010). The school as a microcosm of communities and their heritage and the need to encapsulate this in the writing of school histories. *Yesterday and Today, 5*, 15–21.

Jennings, P.A., & Min, H.H. (2023). Transforming empathy-based stress to compassion: Skillful means to preventing teacher burnout. *Mindfulness*. Springer.

Kahne, J., & Cortes, C.E. (2023). Free speech: Time for a different kind of discussion. *Social Education, 87*(1), 14–21.

Ladson-Billings, G. (2021). I'm here for the hard re-set: Post-pandemic pedagogy to preserve our culture. *Equity & Excellence in Education, 54*(1), 68–78.

Levesque, S., & Croteau, J.P. (2022). "We will continue our struggle for success": French Canadian students, narrative, and historical consciousness. *Theory & Research in Social Education, 50*(1), 101–124.

Matheson, C., & Solomon, E. (Writers), & Parisot, D. (Director). (2020). *Bill & Ted face the music*. Orion Pictures, Endeavor Content, & Hammerstone Studios.

Rogers, M. (2022, November 30). Team USA players share emotional embrace with Iran's Saeid Ezatolahi. *Fox Sports Insider*.

About the Author

Dr. Amber J. Godwin is an assistant professor at the College of Education at Sam Houston State University. She earned her Ph.D. in Curriculum and Instruction from Texas A&M University in 2015. Her research aims to develop critical thinking experiences for learners and explore interventions that enhance social studies education. Prior to entering higher education, she taught AP World History and served as an essay scorer for AP College Board. She contracts with York and National Geographic Learning. In her free time, she enjoys being outside, spontaneous dance parties, and going on adventures with her family and friends.

www.ingramcontent.com/pod-product-compliance
Lightning Source LLC
Chambersburg PA
CBHW020741230426
43665CB00009B/515